CX-ISM

The Philosophy of
Customer Experience

KATIE STABLER

CX-Ism: The Philosophy of Customer Experience

ISBN: 978-1-83709-096-9 (Ebook)
ISBN: 978-1-83709-097-6 (Paperback)
Proofreader: **Alicia Swindells**
Cover Design: CULTIVATE Customer Experience by Design

CX-Ism: The Philosophy of Customer Experience

What's In The Book

Welcome To

CX-ISM

Welcome To CX-Ism

What if the success of your business doesn't lie in your products, services, pricing or marketing? What if it lies in the emotions of each and every one of your customers?

Imagine a world where every interaction and every touchpoint is not just a transaction but a moment of connection.

This isn't a romantic fantasy or a marketing gimmick—it's the reality of business, any business, all businesses, your business.

Welcome to CX-Ism: a philosophy that redefines business success, where customer experience isn't just a strategy you implement—but a movement you lead.

This book contains short, digestible sections focused on particular customer experience-related theories and methodologies to deepen your knowledge of the subject.

We'll journey beyond the buzzwords and superficial tactics to uncover the soul of customer experience—the beliefs, principles, and human truths that turn ordinary businesses into extraordinary ones.

This breadth of understanding is crucial to customer experience (and business) success; it is the catalyst for change and growth, driving customer experience to be the movement it should be.

So often, we do things in business because we think it is the standard. We hold meetings, write reports (so, so many reports), and collect all kinds of data, but why? Customer Experience is no different. Why do we gather feedback? Why do we build personas and map journeys? Why is it all so important?

This book answers that question. It explores the psychology and neuroscience behind customer experience and explains why it is so vital. Armed with that deep understanding, you can enhance your approach to transactional and operational customer experience design and management. More importantly, though, you can develop the essential culture that transforms customer experience from something you have to do to something your organisation believes in intensely. It will no longer be a strategy you implement but a movement you lead.

" —

Choose courage over comfort

— "

Brene Brown

Who should read this book?

Business owners.

Leaders: Not just customer experience leaders, but all business leaders.

Managers who want to make a difference.

Any person at any level who wants to build their knowledge of business success.

It doesn't matter whether you are a solopreneur, the leader of a tiny team, A Customer Service representative, or the CEO of a multinational corporation.

If you want to ensure your business succeeds or simply develop your business and leadership acumen, this book is for you.

How It

Started

How It Started

Let me tell you how I came to be part of the world of customer experience.

Like many, I started on the front line. At the tender age of 14, whilst still at school, dressed in baggy combats and a wallet chain (think skater girl), I began to get my first paychecks; I did all of the typical weekend, cash-in-hand jobs that ambitious youngsters in a seaside town do. I cleaned whelks in a seafood stall on the harbour (enough to put me off eating whelks for life), flipped greasy burgers in the burger stall next door, waited on weekend seaside trippers, and cleaned hundreds of bed and breakfast rooms (I could write an entire book on that experience alone). Gosh, I had fun. Don't get me wrong, as a typical teenager, the early weekend starts were not always easy, and I'm sure my parents had a regular battle to get me out of bed, but looking back, they were some of the best days.

Things only got better, though; upon turning 16, I finally reached the legal age to work in the UK, and so with my national insurance number in hand, I got my first two 'proper jobs', finally earning minimum wage, working in two of Bridlington's staple stores, Woolworths and Boots.

For anyone who predates Gen Z in the UK (born 1995-2012 or earlier), you will be familiar with Woolworths. For those younger or non-native, affectionately known as 'Woolies', Woolworths was a trailblazer in UK retail. Hitting the streets in 1909, Woolies introduced mixed produce stores, where customers could find pretty much anything under one roof.

It was a one-stop shop for household goods and clothing, epitomising affordable goods on the high street. The pick 'n' mix sweets section became a quintessential part of British childhood memories, something every child dreamed of when they walked past the store. One of my personal favourite memories working here was, without a doubt, filling up the pick 'n' mix at the end of each day. Sadly, in 2009, it shut its doors for good. This was long after my departure in 2002, but I sure hope the occasional slip of a pick 'n' mix jelly into my mouth had nothing to do with their financial problems.

At both Woolies and Boots, I revelled in my newfound 'professionalism'. Stocking shelves and serving customers, I loved it all, and I embraced the grown-up feel of clocking in, being in the store before it opened to the public (magic), a work rota, a real payslip and a direct deposit into my bank account each month.

I left my hometown of Bridlington (East Yorkshire, UK) to move to Durham (North East, UK) when I was just 17. I was starting the next phase of my education by heading off to college in an entirely new part of the country, where I knew no one other than the partner I moved with.

This was quite an ambitious step for such a youngster; not only was I starting college, but I stepped onto the property ladder with my first mortgage. This meant that my journey in the world of work needed to continue, and whilst studying, I took on my first call centre role, an industry in which I continued to work throughout my college and university years.

I predominantly worked in sales regarding my life on the phones. his was an entirely new environment from what I'd been used to, and it posed challenges I hadn't experienced in my working life before.

Sales targets, average call handling times, call wrap-up SLAs… language that is now all very familiar but at the time were entirely new concepts. Then there were the call scripts, the call guidelines, the multiple systems and databases to get to grips with, the Data Protection Act (DPA) (now General Data Protection Regulation (GDPR) and regulatory nuance (I primarily worked in finance), not to mention, erm, 'difficult' customers on the other end of what essentially was a cold call (*"IT'S PRONOUNCED COBURN NOT COCKBURN!!"* Oh, sorry, my bad).

However, for each of the challenges these jobs posed, they also offered learning opportunities, confidence building, and growth that were essential as a youngster embarking into that big old world of work. I remember my first call centre interview, I sat at a ridiculously large desk in a pretty bleak room, and the interviewer slid a pen across the desk and, with little explanation, said, "Sell me that pen".

Well, I'd never sold a thing before, and panic flooded me. Still, I pushed my nerves out of the way. I started to highlight all of the positive aspects of the pen, including how it was black and a universally accepted ink colour on formal documentation (I was particularly proud of that point!). I don't know how well I did in this testing torment, but I did get the job, so I guess I did reasonably well.

All of these roles, from the seafood stall on the seafront (pulling sand bags from whelks) to the big call centre in a North East industrial park, had one thing in common: they were all customer-facing, Customer Service roles if you like.

I was preparing myself for a life of customer focus without recognising it at the time. Every interaction taught me about customer behaviour and their wants, needs, and expectations.

Every interaction helped to mould my response to a customer, to adapt to my customers' environment and to recognise where I could do better. Don't get me wrong, I didn't understand this then. I wish my youthful perception was more advanced than it was (I'll try to forgive myself for that, though. Working a 30+ hour week whilst studying for a full-time university degree and with the naivety of youth, no youngster can be blamed for a lacking perception). But, looking back now, I can see the considerable influence these roles had on guiding me to where I am today.

The Career

After my final daily lecture at university, I worked diligently at my contact centre desk, night after night. With a headset attached and bleached by the bright neon lights of the vast room, I started to think about my career. What am I doing all this for, and what will come next?

Honestly, I had **no idea**. I was completing a joint honours in Business Studies and Psychology, a course I enjoyed but had no vocation attached. I couldn't have been more wishy-washy if I'd tried. I think I just picked a course that I thought might give me a good shot at a career (If only I'd have followed my heart and done Music and Drama, perhaps my TV career might have consisted of more than just being a contestant on the UK Masterchef).

There was no such thing as a Customer Experience degree at the time. Even if there were, I doubt I'd have considered it an attractive option, I'd likely have thought it too niche.

I decided that I wanted to work in the not-for-profit sector and do something to help others. So, on top of work and studying, I started to pad out my experience with volunteer work (I really don't know where I found the time and energy, youth I suppose…and a distinct lack of a social life!).

I volunteered for the National Youth Advocacy (NYAS), where I became a friend and mentor to young people experiencing disability.

I also volunteered for the British Red Cross, where I completed a 3-month internship, learning the foundations of not-for-profit admin (and jumping off the side of buildings).

My plan worked, and when I left university, I had a new role waiting for me in the not-for-profit sector. I was ready to start my 'career'. I was to become…**A Capacity Builder**!

What? Yes, a Capacity Builder. It was a new concept to me too, but basically, it involved empowering and up-skilling people experiencing disability in a variety of ways, but most importantly so, giving them a voice (representation) within the Local Authority. I very happily spent several years in this role, and I could write so much about what a wonderful organisation it was, but that wouldn't be the book I've sold to you, so let's get on to the more obvious 'CX' part of the career.

I left that role because I moved from Durham to Cheshire (North West, UK). With a mix of sadness and excitement, I packed up and moved from one green and leafy location to another green and leafy location. I continued my not-for-profit career with a Housing Association, where I worked as a Money Advisor, essentially supporting financially vulnerable people in navigating the welfare and debt system. I loved that job, too (see a theme here?), I would meet people who were stressed and worried, and by the end of my time supporting them, much of their stress and worry was alleviated; it was a humbling and gratifying role.

I'll be honest: I left that job because I was overlooked for a promotion. Sour grapes? No. Well, maybe some. But I knew I wanted more responsibility, and as is always the case, when one door closes, another opens. I had the opportunity to join a debt charity, becoming the Deputy Chief Executive.

It was a glorified title really.

I still undertook the same Money Advice role but with the added responsibility of business administration and regulatory responsibility (Oh, Hello Financial Conduct Authority).

Still, glorified or not, It offered some inspiring opportunities. One of which was the opportunity to speak on the welfare reform in Westminster (a memory I will never forget and possibly the moment where I recognised my love for public speaking), and there's also the fact that I had the pleasure of working with one of my most influential leaders, Nicholas Wulstan Pearson.

The Career: Customer Experience (Finally!)

A few years later, the charity lost funding and with great sadness, and our small but mighty team had to disband.

However, once again, that closed door bumped another open, and my experience afforded me my first, *formally* titled Customer Experience role!

I moved from 'Gatekeeper' to 'Poacher' as I became the Head of Customer Experience for Europe's second-largest credit management company, aka, debt collection company.

Yes, it was an absolute baptism of fire; I led the customer experience function for a company whose customers did not want to be its customers. But, you guessed it, I loved it!

Despite commuting one hundred and twenty miles a day for this role, I worked under another inspirational leader, Sarah Sargent, CX Director at the time, with a fantastic team for a company that really did want to do things in the industry differently.

It wasn't an easy role. There was a lot of persuasion required. I learnt very quickly how important it was to build strong stakeholder relationships, how crucial it was to understand what drove each of them, and how I could use that to build support. What we planned to do here would take a culture change; it needed to be a lasting movement.

Bit by bit, we did just that. We embedded processes that were more than just one-off initiatives, such as Customer Journey Mapping and Impacting Customer Events (ICE), which I'll go into more detail about later in this book.

We created strong governance, including building customer experience into our Quality Assurance (QA) and developing a director-level Customer Experience Forum.

We grew front-line support and engagement with real-time voice of the customer (VoC), including a wrap-around programme of employee reward and recognition.

This involved partnering with a supplier who enabled us to capture customer feedback and sentiment; measure it, analyses it and most importantly, use it to drive positive change across all layers of the organisation.

We shared our actions publicly by being visible at external events, quite a step for an industry shrouded in negative connotations. I went to around the UK, Ireland and even Latvia to share the customer-centric work we were doing in the world of debt collection.

We listened and acted on what our customers said and did, changed our language and behaviour towards them, and started calling them 'Customers' rather than 'Debtors' (a regulation legacy).

Customers started to leave positive reviews online; (can you believe that! Debt Collection company customers left good reviews!) they began to give good feedback, our *NPS increased, they began to engage and interact with us more and debt repayment improved.

That shouldn't have been an industry light bulb moment, but at least it was.

*NPS stands for Net Promotor Score. It's a very common measure across multiple industries which means it is a good benchmarking tool. Whilst I have reservations about NPS use, at the time this company was on such an early journey, using NPS as a customer experience measure gave confidence to some of the harder to engage stakeholders. We thought long and hard about how appropriate it was to ask how likely the customer would be to recommend us (the NPS question) and as strange as it sounds, it did what we needed it to.

You might have spotted that at the beginning of this section, I said I started my first 'formally titled **Customer Experience** role'. I say that because it was. It was the first role I had which included the words 'Customer Experience';but I don't believe it was my first role in customer experience.

Yes, I initially said that I worked in Customer Service roles (my time in Bridlington and Durham), and it should be noted that Customer Service and Customer Experience are not the same. But my time in the not-for-profit companies were, without a shadow of a doubt, customer experience roles too.

No industry is more organically customer-focused than a charity, and my roles within each not-for-profit company that I worked for, concentrated on improving the customer experience that beneficiaries (customers) received. So, once again, my roles, steps, and actions were all building the foundation to become a true customer experience professional.

From there, I became the Director of Customer Experience for a private member organisation and then in 2020, I took the plunge and set up my Customer Experience Consultancy. Since then, I have never looked back.

I've had the pleasure of working around the globe in industries including Telecommunications, Finance, Housing, Local Authority, ICT, SaaS, Airports, Veterinary care, and Quality Assurance. I became a published author and I am frequently listed as one of the top global CX influencers (Number 5 in 2024, thanks to the public votes and professional judges views).

I'm proud to hold the Customer Experience Professionals Association Accreditation (CCXP) and have been fortunate enough to stand on stages worldwide, sharing my passion for the practice of customer experience, including hosting the Awards International, UK Customer Experience Awards.

Back in my university days, if you'd told me I'd end up in Customer Experience, I would've said, 'Say what now?'— as I said, it wasn't even a concept back then.

But today, it's not just a job; it's my calling. It's what drives and excites me, and I can't imagine pouring my heart and energy into anything else. Customer experience is a movement, and it's a movement I am meant to be a part of.

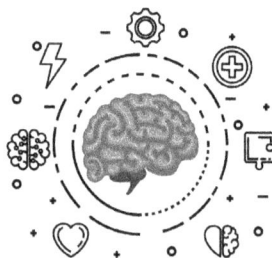

CX

It Isn't A Strategy You Implement But A Movement You Lead

CX: It Isn't A Strategy You Implement But A Movement You Lead

OK, you might be thinking, 'Katie, that's great. You studied, you worked, and you accidentally became a CX-er. So what? What's with the book?'

I'm writing this book because, despite the ever-growing popularity of customer experience, we are still missing a trick. Yes, customer experience has established itself as a must-have business fundamental (alongside the OGs like HR and Finance), but customer satisfaction scores have barely moved an inch.

Twenty (ish) years is relatively young for a business fundamental, presenting a tremendous opportunity to shape the future of customer experience. We will achieve the most significant evolution in customer experience when we truly deeply understand what it is, why it matters, and how we can effectively influence it.

Maya Angelou* once said,

> **"You can't really know where you are going until you know where you have been"**

*Mya Angelou is an American memoirist, poet, and civil rights activist. She became pretty well quoted in the world of CX with this quote, "People will forget what you said. People will forget what you did. But people will never forget how you made them feel", resonating highly with CX professionals

And so, following Maya's advice, before we move onto the philosophy of customer experience, let's take a brief look at its history, particularly its growth and impact.

CX Growth

Expansion of the CX Management Market

The global customer experience management market has experienced substantial growth, valued at USD 12.04 billion in 2023, with projections to reach USD 32.87 billion by 2030 (data collected between 2018 and 2023). Their research highlights that this growth can be attributed to the rising importance of understanding customer behaviour and their preferences, which drives companies to implement customer experience strategies**. The increasing use of digital technology is expected to produce optimised use of artificial intelligence (AI), cloud technology and work collaboration tools, subsequently extrapolating customer experience management (CEM) market growth. (Grand View Research)

Dedicated CX Departments: According to the Technology and Services Industry Association, 51% of the technology and services companies they surveyed in 2024 have established dedicated customer experience departments, over and above the traditional customer success functions.

**Customer Experience Management Market Size Report 2030. https://www.grandviewresearch.com/industry-analysis/customer-experience-management-market

Prioritisation of CX In Business Strategies

Following on from dedicated CX departments, a survey by SuperOffice revealed that customer experience is a top priority for businesses, surpassing product and pricing considerations. 1,920 business professionals (46%) identified CX as the foremost priority for the next five years. This is fantastic to see as research from the likes of Qualtrics (2024) shows this aligns with customers prioritising customer service alongside price and quality.

The Emergence Of Specialised CX Roles

Taking responsibility for CX prioritisation, today, most companies report having a chief experience officer or its equivalent, although that person's responsibilities, decision rights, and metrics of success are still emerging, according to a 2024 Deloitte survey of 250 customer experience leaders. This uncertainty of defined responsibility is likely down to 50% of respondents being the first in their organisation to serve as an experience leader, underscoring just how emerging this senior-level role is.

Financial Impact Of CX Investments

We can't forget to include return on investment here; the ROI of resources always has its place. What's in it for us? Well, quite a lot, actually; research by The Temkin Group shows that companies earning 1 billion dollars annually can expect to earn, on average, an additional $700 million within 3 years of investing in their customer experience.

OK, you might not have a 1 billion dollars (£792,300.000.00 sterling, 2024 conversion rate) to chuck at customer experience.

Still, the story's moral is that brands with outstanding customer experience generate 5.7 times more revenue than competitors who lag in this department.*

Collectively, these developments demonstrate the substantial growth and establishment of customer experience as a critical component of business strategy over the past 20 years, yet despite these investments, overall customer satisfaction has not seen a corresponding increase. Why?

Declining Customer Satisfaction Scores

Until 2024, The American Customer Satisfaction Index (ACSI) reported continually low scores with a downturn to 73.4/100 in 2022, reflecting the possible impact of COVID-19. Although in 2024, July's data showed a near-record level of 77.9, the UK wasn't so fortunate, with a declining score of 75.8.

I'm only skimming the surface here; this list could go on and on. I bet you're thinking of adding a few points as we speak. The critical takeaway point here is that while the focus on customer experience has intensified, achieving a proportional increase in customer satisfaction proves to be elusive.

*40+ Statistics That Highlight the Importance of Customer Experience. https://www.edume.com/blog/customer-experience-statistics?hs_amp=true

Disappointingly so.

Company crushingly so.

And I am confident that I know why. You might think that scores in the 70s range don't seem too dismal, so let me put these scores into context. The ACSI was established in 1994, and the first score reported was 74.8.

The UK Customer Satisfaction Index (UKCSI) was first published in January 2008, and in 2010 it reported the UK's lowest score of 75.8.

Do you read this and feel dubious about the data? How can it be so? So much effort for such little reward.

If you are dubious, here's a third data point for you. Forrester's Customer Experience Index 2024 revealed that U.S. customer experience quality declined for the third consecutive year, reaching its lowest point since 2016. The average score dropped from 72.0 in 2021 to 69.3 in 2024.

Sorry to be the bearer of that news.

Although presented in simple data, the reality behind it is far more complex. There isn't one definitive reason why we haven't seen the increases in customer happiness and satisfaction that businesses investing in customer experience would hope to see. There are a variety of factors that contribute to the gap between investment and result, a couple of which are:

- **Rising Customer Expectations:** As companies enhance their CX efforts, customer expectations may have escalated concurrently, making achieving higher satisfaction levels more challenging.

- **Inconsistent Implementation of CX Strategies:** Despite best intentions, not all organisations have effectively executed CX initiatives, leading to varied customer experiences and, in some cases, dissatisfaction (Step in CX-Ism!).

- **Technological Challenges**: The rapid adoption of technologies and AI-powered solutions has resulted in some underdeveloped solutions being deployed, causing customer frustration. Something I believe will happen more frequently in the near future.

- **Under-Resourced Initiatives:** There isn't a quick way of achieving excellent customer experience, and there isn't an end point where a company can say, 'tick, done.' Yet some customer experience budgets would make you think otherwise.

Customer experience shouldn't be just a strategy you implement but a movement you lead. Its value to the business is paramount yet often misunderstood, under appreciated and thus under-resourced.

Time and time again, I see companies needing to recognise the transformative power of customer experience and the cultural commitment required.

This outstanding need ultimately leads to underperformance in the areas listed above, to name but a few.

So this book is aimed at challenging our understanding of customer experience, going deeper than you may have been before, delving underneath superficial tactics to uncover the soul of customer experience—the beliefs, the principles, and the human truths that turn ordinary businesses into extraordinary ones.

Let's get started.

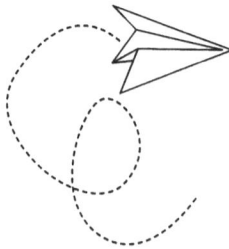

Perception

A Core Understanding

Perception: A Core Understanding

Scientifically speaking, perception is the process of individual interpretation of ambiguous sensory signals that we take in from the world around us. We transform these signals into objects, people, places, and feelings—the tangible and intangible things that make up our reality.

There are many theories on the neurology of consciousness and perception, which, like most scientific theories, have evolved as science and technology have progressed.

After 20 years of researching the brain, world-renowned neuroscientist Professor Anil Seth has a radical new theory on consciousness. It includes an evolved view of perception as an inside-out process, a hypothesis coined 'Controlled Hallucinations'. When I first read about this in his groundbreaking book, **Being You**, I understood that this theory could be a very useful tool for understanding, gauging, and ultimately, improving customer experiences (and it quickly became one of my favourite books; a place for constant inspiration).

Professor Seth theorises that our brains aren't cameras; they're creators. We don't passively view reality; we actively build it, filling in gaps with our own expectations and experiences. This is useful, though only sometimes perfectly accurate. It has big implications for how we understand ourselves, others, experiences, and even reality itself.

So Why Is This Important In CX?

Because we can each **experience** the same thing yet *perceive* it very differently. Your customer service nightmare could be another person's walk in the park!

This is obvious, of course. To all of you reading this, it should make absolute sense. It's practically a given, right? Well, yes. At least, it's a given in our worlds outside of business.

However, let's step into the proverbial office for a moment. Too many companies still fail to focus enough on understanding the nuances of what they **think** their customer experience is compared to their customers' *reality*, the customers actual *perception* of the experience.

When discussing customer experience, businesses often focus on metrics, A/B tests, and efficiencies. Although these data-driven approaches can and do yield valuable insights, Professor Seth's work on consciousness and perception offers a compelling shift in our own perspective, namely:

Customer experience isn't just about optimising interactions; it's about understanding the conscious canvas on which those interactions paint a lasting perception.

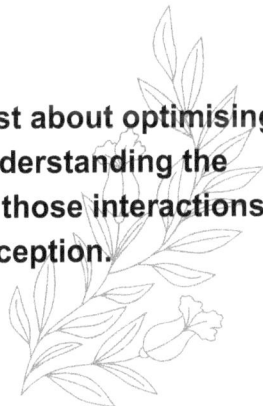

How Does This Apply In the Real World of CX?

OK, consider this. Mrs Customer has an annoying journey trying to purchase something from your website.

The data and metrics you use to assure the customer experience might show that she navigated the website exactly as the company expected. She walked through all the steps you designed and reached her outcome.

Meanwhile, Mrs Customer's own expectations of the site and the steps she needed to go through differed significantly from the experience you believe you have delivered. Her perception is, therefore, significantly different from what your company's data suggests.

Your business's perceived ease of purchase depends not just on the user flow but also on Mrs Customer's mental model, and this is what many companies overlook.

Your customer's mental model can be determined by many factors, such as their past experiences with similar interfaces, their past experience with you and even their current emotional state. A simple website design (or any design element of the customer experience) might miss the mark if it doesn't consider the user's subjective world.

Put Theory Into Practice

So, what can we learn from Professor Seth's theory? I see at least three clear lessons:

Embrace Emotion As A Driver Of Perception

Along with many others, Professor Seth emphasises the role of emotions in shaping our experiences.

A stressed customer navigating a complex system will perceive every step as arduous, regardless of its objective ease. We need to recognise that emotion plays a significant part in how the customer perceives their interaction.

Building intentional emotional connections through empathetic language, positive reinforcement, and even subtle design cues can significantly alter the perceived experience.

Empathise With The "Why"

Metrics offer a "what," but understanding the "why" requires considering the user's mental model.

Eye-tracking, surveys, and even well-designed open-ended questions can help unveil the user's internal map and expectations.

For example, a high bounce rate on a product page might not be about bad visuals or a glitch on the website but about a perceived mismatch between the advertised product and the user's expectations.

Design For Anticipation, Not Just Reaction

Predicting user needs and addressing them before they arise not only reduces customer's cognitive load but also fosters a sense of control and satisfaction. Proactive suggestions, personalised information, and intuitive interfaces that "read" the customer's intent can significantly enhance the perceived ease and flow of interaction.

Professor Seth's groundbreaking theory, while not explicitly about customer experience, has important implications for the practice of CX. It underscores the need to understand that customer experience is not only about optimising interactions but also about understanding and shaping the user's subjective reality.

By acknowledging the "predictive brain" and considering the conscious canvas upon which experiences unfold, businesses can cultivate meaningful connections, foster positive perceptions, and drive genuine customer loyalty.

This is just a taster. As I said, Professor Seth's work is a place of inspiration and insights that you can embrace to level up their customer experience game. By understanding the complexity of consciousness and perception and utilising it in operational design, we can move beyond the oppression of metrics and create truly transformative customer experiences.

Perception

The Peak End Rule

Perception: The Peak End Rule

I couldn't write a book about customer experience, focusing so heavily on perception and emotion, and fail to recognise the work of the late and great Daniel Kahneman. Daniel Kahneman was an esteemed Psychologist and Nobel laureate (Nobel Prize winner) who passed away in 2024 at the age of ninety. His legacy will live on through his pioneering work in behavioural economics and cognitive psychology, more of which I will be touching on in subsequent chapters. But I'd like to start with the **Peak End Rule.**

The Peak End Rule is a psychological principle that underscores that two parts of the experience shape our overall perception of an experience: the peak and the end.

The peak of an experience refers to the moments that are most emotionally impactful, the most intense parts of the experience, good or bad.

The end of the experience needs little explanation, but it is the final part of the experience.

This finding was (and still is) significant for experience designers because it demonstrates that the duration or totality of an experience has less lasting impact on the customer than the emotional highlights or end of the experience. Yes, we are following on from our start with Professor Seth and continuing to talk about emotion.

If you are already a keen CX-er, behavioural economist, or have an interest in cognitive psychology, then you may be familiar with the Peak End Rule. However, did you know what research took place to achieve this finding?

The research primarily involved experiments where discomfort or pain was involved; it explored how people remembered these experiences, and one critical experiment helped lead to the discovery of the Peak End Rule: The 1990 colonoscopy.

Patients underwent the colonoscopy, and as they did, they were asked to use a scale to rate their pain and discomfort levels. Afterwards, they were also asked to evaluate the whole experience and detail how uncomfortable or painful they considered it to be. The procedures were different; some patients experienced a shorter procedure with a more painful end, and others a more prolonged procedure with a less painful end. The findings were disproportionately influenced by (you guessed it!) the most intense moments of pain (the peak) and the levels of pain at the end of the procedure (the end).

Kahneman and his colleagues also discovered the Duration Neglect Phenomenon during this research. Despite a more prolonged procedure, participants would rate their experience more positively if the ending was less painful.

Essentially, this highlighted that the duration of the experience mattered much less than the key moments.

So we are looking at the relatively simple baseline theory that if we design positive emotional peaks into the experience, try and reduce any harmful emotion-invoking elements and create a pleasant ending, we will have a relatively good shot at creating the perception of a good customer experience.

This is where intentional customer experience design and management come into play. You see, it's doubtful that any of us wake up in the morning and say, "I'm going to design a terrible customer experience today'. No, that is extreme and quite counterproductive. But, few of us look beyond the basics (follow this user pathway, make sure this button works, yes, the IVR is up and running, and the wait time is sub sixty seconds) and actually design a customer experience using solid theories and principles like Professor Seths and Kahneman's.

Few, but not none.

Let's take a look at Ikea.

Love it or hate it, you wander through the maze of rooms, picking up bits and pieces and maybe some design inspiration, then, plonked right in the middle, is the restaurant where you can fill your belly and warm your heart with the famous Ikea meatballs! Good peak.

Then, you make your way to the warehouse. Ikea says your item is in stock, but when you get to your lettered aisle and numbered shelf, the item is nowhere to be seen.

You find it dumped nearby and drag it on your dodgy-wheeled trolly to the checkout. Bad peak.

You finally get through, and just before you leave, you get tempted by the frozen meatball takeaway option and let the kids get the £1 ice creams. A happy ending.

While there are some negative peaks, these are often parts of the experience that (to a degree) are out of Ikea's total control. However, thoughtfully designed positive peaks might just be enough to tip the balance in Ikea's favour regarding memory, perception, and, ultimately, customer experience.

While Ikea doesn't explicitly detail anywhere that they use the Peak End Rule, it's not past the realm of possibility that a company that invests so much into design haven't leaned into this principle to support its success.

Another example of the Peak End Rule in practice is to think about any car service you have ever had. You get to the garage and expect to wait a few hours whilst your car is being serviced; you use the free wifi and take advantage of the complimentary drinks machine (peak); you start to get a bit bored of waiting, and there's a nice big bill to pay, but when you drive out of the car park, you revel in the lovely smelling, freshly valeted interior (happy end).

These aren't joyful mishaps; they are smartly designed experiences.

Put Theory Into Practice

Like with Professor Seth's theory, let me provide some practical actions you can take concerning the Peak End Rule.

Embrace Emotion (Again): We will get emotion into the board room! Wink.

We have to astutely recognise the emotions a customer feels during their experience with our business because emotion influences the perception the customer creates. Whether it's happiness, joy, surprise, sadness, frustration or anger, the peaks that stir emotions are what create memory nodes and will determine how customers remember us (and how they talk about us).

Did you know that, by and large, we don't remember an actual event that happened; we remember the memory of that event? Our brains don't directly play back memories like a recording; instead, they reconstruct them (as Professor Seth says, our brains aren't cameras; they are creators). We use fragments of information to build what we consider a memory, and guess what? The fragments that we will most likely remember and recall are those glowing with the heat of emotion.

Design Peaks And A Happy Ending

Don't leave experience peaks to chance; review your customer experience and consider where you can inject some high-impact positive emotion.

Likewise, ensure your customer leaves that interaction on a good note.

Impactful peaks don't necessarily have to be real surprise and delight moments, although some companies do that well.

In the US, the budget hotel chain Magic Castle offers a Popsicle Hotline where guests can order free ice lollies, and the hotel staff delivers them with a white glove service- fun!

But you don't have to start giving away ice lollies or any other freebies, a peak can be something as simple as a customer receiving a personalised welcome email from you when they sign up.

Purdy & Figg offer a great example of this. They are a non-toxic cleaning produce company, but they describe themselves as a community of people switching to simple, natural cleaning (Big love to that!). As a new customer, you receive an email which:

- **Thanks you.** It's not an order confirmation, where an obligatory thank you is plonked in the text. This is a welcome email, and first and foremost, they want to thank you for supporting them.

- **Tells you their story:** It's not a self-indulgent prologue that takes a whole coffee to read, but in four sentences, they succinctly shared their humble origin and company ambition.

- **Prioritise customer support:** They dedicate a short paragraph to their customer support and how, if needed, you can access it.

Let's be honest. This e-mail is not brain science, nor does it take inhuman effort to design and automate. But it is sincere, authentic and personal and most importantly, it creates sentiment, the peak, which is an absolute must for customer loyalty.

And the all-important interaction end does not have to be an all-singing, all-dancing affair (although it can be if that's your thing).

Instead, it can be as simple as ensuring the checkout process is smooth and easy. For example, imagine indulging in a carefree walk around a store during your lunch break, picking up a few items you don't need and heading to the checkout. If there is a long queue, a cold draft coming through the open doors and a check-out assistant seems entirely disinterested in being there, then the enjoyment you felt from a lunchtime treat might quickly dissipate, and you may dump the items and ditch the store. However, if you get to the check-out, the queue reduces quickly, and the assistant is really friendly, loves your hat and asks where you got it, you will likely leave that interaction on a high and find yourself back there later in the week.

Cleverly designing with the Peak End Rule isn't tricky; it just requires a good understanding of your customer's experience and a little time and effort.

Recognise The Opportunity A Negative Peak Creates

We are aspiring for an experience full of positive peaks, but let's face it, we can't always avoid bad things happening.

Think back to the example from Ikea for a moment. The trolly with a dodgy wheel might not get noticed by staff for a while, and the in-stock item nowhere to be found could be the result of a customer not placing an item back in the right place and, again, not correcting it before it impacts another customer. These occurrences may create a negative peak and simply aren't always avoidable.

Whether our people, technology or process fail us, there is always a chance that something could go wrong; heck, even external factors can influence our business and the subsequent customer experience we deliver (sorry to mention it again, but COVID-19 would be a prime example of that).

But for everything that goes wrong, there is an opportunity to flip it on its head and create a positive peak; there's the opportunity to create an even more emotionally engaged customer. So it is essential to try and recognise your customer experience areas of risk and design to try and prevent them where possible, or where prevention isn't a certainty, at least recover the experience.

There is a whole chapter on this, so if you can't wait until you reach it, head to page....to read about the Customer Service Recovery Paradox.

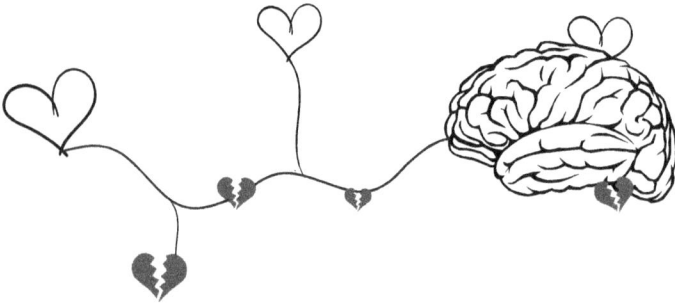

Perception

Loss Aversion

Perception: Loss Aversion

Emotions matter. Have I said that enough?

The peak moments of an interaction or journey, the most emotionally evocative, create a memory, a lasting impression, a perception.

It makes sense that the more negative emotions that are stirred and the more negative peaks that are created, we, as customers, are much less likely to return to that brand.

But Why?

Because we have evolved to protect ourselves, where once upon a time, in a challenging terrain, dressed in nothing but our birthday suits, if we heard a grizzly noise coming from the depths of a cave, we would likely activate self-preservation mode and make a mental note to stay away from that cave for a while.

Yes, we could take a chance to hunt the suspected animal lurking and, if successful, feed the clan. Maybe it isn't a bear, and the hunt will be a doddle, or perhaps it is a bear, but we still manage to take it down. But no, we will likely err on the side of caution, and we will let sleeping bears lie; we'll check on the rabbit trap instead.*

*Please don't contact me about what is probably a highly inaccurate depiction of a Homo Sapiens, I acknowledge that I'm rusty in that area, and this is a purely fictional analogy

We generally have fewer bears in caves to worry about now. Instead, we have scary customer experiences to protect ourselves from. After a few negative interactions, even if we really want that product or service, we won't put ourselves through another ordeal; we will simply go without or go elsewhere.

This behaviour can be attributed to **Loss aversion**.

Loss aversion is the tendency to avoid a loss in scenarios with the potential for an equivalent gain. Imagine you are playing a game where you can continue to play and will either win £300 or lose £150, or you could end the game now without money coming into it at all. Much like our Homo Sapiens ancestors will likely leave the bear cave alone, most of us would end the game, choosing not to risk losing money despite the potential win being double that of the loss.

This is because we have a cognitive bias where the psychological pain of losing is twice as impactful and twice as painful as the pleasure of gaining.

In the world of customer experience, this cognitive bias makes customers air on the side of caution, choosing to operate conservatively to protect themselves from the pain of a repeatedly poor experience instead of benefiting from the pleasure of getting what they want.

This is why risk-free trials work so well. Have you downloaded an app recently or started a subscription that offers you a free trial? Would you have downloaded that app or started that subscription if you couldn't' test it first? Many of us wouldn't because we wouldn't want to run the risk that the app or subscription doesn't quite meet our expectations, and then we would be out of pocket.

By offering a free trial, companies reduce the customers perceived risk of loss and thus removes the need for the customer's cognitive bias to kick in.

Much like with the free trials, there are actually many ways that risk aversion can work in a company's favour if you understand how to utilise it and design the experience around this cognitive bias.

Put Theory Into Practice

Let's look at the ways you can design with loss aversion in mind.

Understand How Purchase Decisions Are Made

Significant research has taken place over the years, demonstrating that we are more likely to make decisions that enable us to avoid a loss rather than gain something.

Anecdotally, as I write this, I am awaiting the delivery of a new Macbook; I purchased it because my current four-year-old model has been running slowly for a while, and despite best clean-up efforts, I fear it is on the fritz. The purchase decision of a new Macbook was not made based on any excitement or reward (it's essentially the same piece of kit that I already have) but out of fear of the old one going kaput at any time—loss aversion at its best.

Understanding how cognitive bias influences customers' decisions enables you to use it to your advantage. For example, highlight loss avoidance; when purchasing the new Macbook, I was about to check out with the cheapest option in my cart when I was presented with some upgrade options. These upgrades included more significant memory, which would protect me against some of the issues I am facing with my current model (which has the lowest memory available, a past purchase naivety on my part).

Use Loss Aversion to Nurture Loyalty

It always struck me as incredibly strange when companies offer new customer discounts. Still, when an annual renewal comes around for customers, the prices get hiked. This is most commonly seen in industries like insurance, TV and broadband (not all companies!). The sceptic in me believes it's because those companies rely on customers not noticing and unwittingly entering into a more pricey contract. Let me tell you, there's no better way to lose a customer than to make them feel undervalued and ripped off.

Loss aversion tells us we should be doing the opposite. We should offer price guarantees, loyal customer discounts and loyalty programmes, all things which emphasise a loss if the customer were to leave.

The loss of the price guarantee, the loss of the loyal customer status and the loss of the rewards. These losses should play a part in your customer's decision-making process and likely lead to them sticking around a little longer.

Use Loss Aversion To Improve Customer Retention

Loss aversion use is a tactic that should come into full use when a customer finally decides to leave you, and you have likely experienced this yourself. Think about the last subscription you ended. Were you faced with page after page of offers?

"Can we entice you to stay with three months at half price?". **No**

"What about six months' half price?". **No**

"We will come round and bake you an apple pie?" **No**

"Are you sure?"

Okay, perhaps they don't go quite that far, but typically,

companies entice you with these special offers that they know you don't need (because you have already made that decision to leave) in the hope that the idea of losing these 'deals' makes you stay a little longer.

Offering customers something they will find hard to decline through fear of missing out (FOMO) is a well-used retention strategy, although it must be used cautiously.

Too much friction at the end of a customer journey (e.g., difficulty cancelling because the cancellation page is nigh on impossible to find, you have to call to cancel, or there are 101 offers you need to decline first) will stomp on any loss aversion behavioural benefits and just cause frustration, giving your customer a helping hand out of the door.

Understand How Loss Aversion Creates Frustration and Complaints

Whilst loss aversion is valuable to understand with respect to customer purchasing behaviour and perceived 'loyalty', it is also really helpful to keep in mind when it comes to customer dissatisfaction and complaints.

Think about what I wrote above, *"the psychological pain of losing is twice as impactful and twice as painful as the pleasure of gaining."*. When we lose out in some way, we feel it, and it hurts, leading to annoyance, frustration, even anger (Peak End Rule anyone?), and maybe a complaint.

A customer could be impacted by loss aversion if they feel

they have **lost money**: I paid over £600 for a business-related subscription that did not have a free trial (rookie mistake on my side), and upon use, I quickly found out that it didn't meet my needs whatsoever, so within twenty-four hours, and with a demonstrable lack of use, I emailed them to explain and kindly ask for a refund.

They were quick to deny me, and due to it being a business subscription, my consumer rights didn't apply, and well, I lost that money.

Boy, did that hurt! I really felt it, and whilst I didn't complain (they hadn't done anything wrong, although I do question their judgement on that policy), I felt hugely aggrieved, I most certainly won't be resubscribing, and if asked by someone in my network, I would likely actively warn others against the subscription.

It doesn't always come down to money, a customer could experience loss aversion through a **loss of trust.** In a later chapter on captive customers, I discuss my brand captivity (perceived loyalty) with a well-known, high-end audio technology company.

After years of custom, this company let me down on the product quality and customer service front (a double whammy). I lost trust in them, and again, it hurt. After years of faithful patronage, I felt let down, and in this instance, I absolutely did complain (it was a sham of a complaints process, however. A total waste of time and another let down).

Then there's **time**. Time is one of our most valuable assets, and customers, I would say, most commonly experience loss aversion when they lose their precious time in interacting with a company.

Consider this scenario: You have a problem and spend some time troubleshooting it yourself but get nowhere fast.

You know this is one of those problems where you are more likely to get it sorted if you speak with a real person, so you spend some more time trying to find a phone number, and then you call.

You find yourself in a queue listening to crackly music (how is that still happening?) that is interrupted too frequently by a voice telling you that your call is important. Some time much later, you speak to someone, you don't get the solution you hoped for, and over the course of the week, there are subsequent calls and emails before an outcome is finally reached.

Does that feel familiar? I think we have all been there, and the most significant source of frustration and upset is not the delayed outcome but the amount of time we feel we are unnecessarily wasting on something we absolutely shouldn't be spending so much time on.

So, we must understand the significance of loss, not only in how it affects customers' purchasing decisions but also in how a perceived loss impacts our relationship with that customer.

We generally have fewer bears in caves to worry about now. Instead, we have scary customer experiences to protect ourselves from.

Listen

To The Layers Of Meaning

Listen To The Layers Of Meaning

Are you familiar with the musician Hrishikesh Hirway? If not, take 10 minutes now to find him on whichever music streaming service you use. Download a song and listen before you continue to read; listen fully, without distraction (a favourite of mine is Between There and Here. I'm listening to it right now, although, obviously, with distraction).

I came across Hrishikesh when he delivered a beautiful and thought-provoking TedTalk in 2021 entitled 'What you discover when you really listen'—revolving around music and communication, leaning into the idea that sitting behind what people say, there are layers of meaning that form by the context of what we experience (sound familiar to some of what we have already discussed?).

Whilst Hrishikesh's Ted Talk had nothing explicitly to do with customer experience, I listened and tingled. The concepts he shared are paramount in the world of customer experience; I mean, the title alone screams customer experience, 'What you discover when you really listen'. Our customers talk to us, give us feedback, make complaints, and give us praise, but how often do we look beyond the surface level of this information to understand what drives it? Do we really listen?

Does that feel familiar? I think we have all been there, and the most significant source of frustration and upset is not the delayed outcome but the amount of time we feel we are unnecessarily wasting on something we absolutely shouldn't be spending so much time on.

So, we must understand the significance of loss, not only in how it affects customers' purchasing decisions but also in how a perceived loss impacts our relationship with that customer.

The ability to listen is a seriously underrated quality, and it's a skill that not all businesses have mastered. Despite the many channels, tools, and technology available to enable us to really hear what our customers are telling us, we still often just skim the surface. If we do manage to listen and understand, then we usually fall into the second trap that Hrishikesh discusses: we turn the focus inward rather than hold it firmly on them.

The ability to listen can be the catalyst for cultivating satisfied and loyal customers or creating a level of frustration that customers can only be relieved by walking away.

So why do we still fall short here when listening to our customers is so invaluable?

Put Theory Into Practice

Stop Ignoring The Context

Hearing the context is essential because the actual root cause may lead to different experience-enhancement actions.

For example, we might hear customers in mortgage arrears complaining about waiting in call queues.

At face value, these remarks relate to dissatisfaction regarding long hold times, but at the core, these customers may be worried and anxious about the pending call, and so any wait time, long or short, may lead to feelings of dissatisfaction (emotion driving perception once again).

In this instance, increasing customer satisfaction may have nothing to do with call hold times, but the contact we make before their contact, the website and IVR message or even the self-service options available here may have a more significant influence on satisfaction.

Our actions to make the customer feel understood, supported, and in control are more important than how long the customer must wait on hold. Context is important.

Stop Moving the Focus From the Customer to the Business

Have you ever heard the phrase 'Be obsessed with the problem, not the solution'?

It relates to an issue that companies often face, in that we have great ideas to fix or improve things for our customers, and we become laser-focused on bringing these ideas to life, but we don't always consider if it's the best course of action for the customer experience.

In Hrishikesh's talk, he shares how a common communication pitfall is the temptation to turn the focus of the conversation onto us and again, in the world of customer experience, I see this happen frequently. We might see and hear the customer feedback, but our bias makes us respond in a way that is more about us than about them.

A prevalent example of this occurrence is digital channel shifts. I've seen companies hear their customers' plea to make contact more straightforward and quicker, but instead of working to understand their customers' actual needs and build a suitable omnichannel experience, the company has turned inward and opted for the easiest/cheapest/fastest solution instead.

In one instance, I saw a housing association use WhatsApp as its predominant self-service channel. It quickly belly-flopped (at a high cost) due to the older demographic needing a more comfortable and relevant channel of choice.

On the face of it, WhatsApp may seem like a progressive communication option, but as a vast percentage of the population was not WhatsApps target age, it simply wasn't the right channel of choice.

Create Curiosity

I'm not referring to individual curiosity here; I'm referring to institutional curiosity, supported by the kind of culture in which an organisation is always learning (in this instance, about its customers).

Curiosity is the conduit to understanding and listening to our customers; it prompts us to ask questions, dig into unknowns, and discover everything we can about what makes our customers tick.

This kind of institutional curiosity takes time, effort and, ultimately, enablement. Teams need to be supported to be inquisitive, and one of the biggest challenges to developing this culture is the perpetual lack of time as they battle against daily firefighting.

Immerse Yourself In The Customer Experience

We can listen to our customers in many ways–including social media, direct feedback, complaints, repeat purchases, frontline teams, and conversational analytics. All these insight sources tell us something, and the list could go on.

The challenge comes in actually pulling all of these data points together and looking at insight as a whole.

Ultimately, the more we listen to our customers, the more we understand what they experience, expect, and want. This knowledge is the foundation for what comes next.

This knowledge enables insight-driven action, so organisations need to be prepared and equipped to use this insight to act.

Our customers have so much to tell us, whether through their words or actions. We need to truly listen, hold the focus on them and explore beyond what lies on the surface.

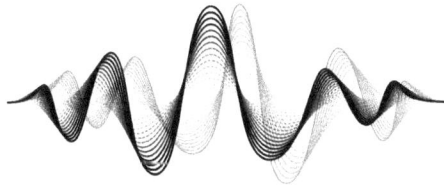

> "The pictures that I've framed
> Don't tell the stories in between
> The moments that contain
> Who you really were to me"

"Between There and Here" by Hrishikesh
Hirway featuring

Captive

Customers

Captive Customers

When you are creating your Customer Personas*, do you consider if they are a Captive Customer? I'm going to take a guess and say you don't. Well, maybe you should, and this section will convince you.

I coined the term Captive Customer a number of years ago when I worked as the head of customer experience for Europe's second-largest credit management company, a.k.a, debt collection**.

As you can imagine, our customers did not want to be our customers, nobody ever woke up and said, "I'm not going to pay my bills today because I'd love to become a debt collection company customer!". No, instead, for many, being a customer of a debt collection company is something that creates worry, even fear, it sadly is still shrouded in stigma and shame (and I wholeheartedly support the advances that many in the industry are striving to make to change that).

Nonetheless, despite literally nobody wanting to be our customer, we had customers. A lot of them. 3.5 million, in fact, since the company opened its doors in 2007.

*Customer personas are a great tool to help you understand and contextualise your customers' wants and needs; they are not just a marketing tool. If you aren't using them, why not? I won't cover them in detail in this book, but a quick Google search will give you all the information you need to get started, or you can, of course, contact CULTIVATE for help.
**If you knew of this term before me, that would be great. I'd be pleased to follow the steps of the astute.

These are the epitome of a Captive Customer, they didn't opt to be a customer, they didn't want to be a customer, they have no choice in whether to be a customer and when they can clear their liability, they definitely don't want to be a returning customer***.

A Captive Customer is, as the name suggests, a captive. They don't particularly want to be your customer, but for some reason, they lack options, and they are yours through necessity, their 'choice' is non-existent or forced.

Debt collection customers are an easy but extreme example. If you are not familiar with the world of debt collection, when you have a debt that is being managed by a debt collection company, you do not get to choose which company manages that debt (your original creditor is responsible for that).

Few other Captive Customers are that clear-cut. In the UK, you could say that patients (customers) of the NHS are captive because you have to use the local GP and dentist you are registered with. Water companies, too, have a Captive Customer base. As a residential customer (at least in the UK), you have no choice but to pay water rates to the company that looks after the water provision in your part of the country.

***There is a caveat to this. This company actually became pretty good at showing customers that they care and making it easy for customers to interact with and manage their debts. This resulted in a Net Promoter Score (NPS) of 54 in 2023, and I remember partaking in customer interviews whilst working there, in which customers said that if they could choose this debt collection company over others, they would. So, unsurprisingly, it really did pay to concentrate on customer experience in this industry.

Yet despite few industries so overtly hosting Captive Customers, customers can experience captivity for a number of reasons.

Cost Captivity

Airlines are a great example of cost captivity.

Customers may use budget-friendly airlines to keep travel costs down, favouring keeping their holiday money for the holiday rather than paying extra for a flight with a few more bells and whistles.

Mrs customer may not really want to fly with Wing and A Prayer Airlines ("We'll get you there…probably!"), but if she wants those extra nightly spicy margaritas at the swim-up bar, that's the price she has to pay.

Budget supermarkets are another typical cost captivity example. When the pennies are pinched, the average consumer looks to save money on household spending and resorts to budget-friendly supermarkets. Did you know that, shockingly, according to Which, one in six people reported skipping meals due to soaring food costs in 2023? So, it is no surprise to see people seeking more affordable options.

However, it is less straightforward with supermarkets, as even affluent households appreciate value for money, especially when it comes to non-differentiated items which see little quality change, regardless of where they are purchased (particularly economic turbulent times).

Location Captivity

I recall listening to a podcast, an episode of Customer Experience Superheroes, by Christopher Brooks (bookmark to listen to later). During this particular episode, Dr Phil Klaus, Professor of Customer Experience Strategy at the International University of Monaco, was a guest. Imagine how my ears pricked when he shared research that referenced captive customers.

Dr Klaus shared how a loyal customer frequented a local car garage, however, when interviewed, it came to light that what was mistaken for loyalty was actually a necessity as this garage turned out to be the only one within the customer's required vicinity. He was not frequenting the garage out of choice but because he had no choice.

So, location can be a creator of customer captivity. Just take a second to think about the local store you shop at, perhaps you live in a town, and you have options galore at your fingertips. I, however, live in a village with one shop, and although the shop is a perfectly fine, well-known chain of convenience stores, I would choose to shop at an independent retailer if that choice was available.

Product Captivity

In this instance, customers can be captive because of the need for a very specific product or service that presents limited purchase options.

For example, you might be the proud owner of an ECOVACS DEBOT (a floor hoovering and mopping robot one can simply not live without), which requires ECOVACS parts and accessories to be purchased directly from ECOVACS.

This isn't a fictional mop bot. It's the brand I have (much needed when you have a furry beast the size of a small pony roaming the house) and yes, I am captive to the brand parts and accessories.

Brand Captivity

Otherwise known as loyalty (said with a wry smile).

What is customer loyalty other than a customer being captivated by a brand, drawn in and holding tight the the belief that no other phone brand, kitchen mixer brand, trainer brand, etc, is better than the brand they have committed time and money to.

But we have all had that moment where we break free of brand captivity, and our brand loyalty dissipates for some reason, be it the competition just progressing light-years quicker or your much-loved brand slapping you in the face with a wet fish (metaphorically.)

For me, that wet fish slap came after years of buying all of my audio technology from my favourite, well-known, high-end brand.

I purchased some new earbuds, and after a week of joyful, super-crisp sound, they stopped working. Sad times, but that wasn't the wet fish slap.

It was the Customer Service that left me disappointed; they seemed to care little and know even less, and although my products were under warranty and would be replaced, that process would take over three weeks.

This, however, was still not the wet fish slap.

I received my replacement buds, and although they lasted slightly longer, after just a few months, they, too, went kaput.

This time, I decided I wasn't prepared to wait another three weeks for a replacement with clearly failing technology, so I requested a refund. The refund was granted, but rather than being refunded £279.99, the price of the earbuds, I received a refund of £27.99. Now, I don't claim to be all-knowing, but it seems to me that a relatively straightforward admin mistake was made; someone misplaced the decimal place, right?

But no, apparently, it wasn't so straightforward, and it took a whole month of me chasing this company and playing along to their silly requests before I finally received the full refund.

There's the wet fish slap, and there's the dissipated brand loyalty.

If you do have a Captive Customer, whether through cost, location, product or brand captivity you might be tempted to think, 'Great', they are my customers, and by hook or crook, they are here to stay. Woohoo.

But this view is a mistake because if we take captive customers for granted, we may pay less attention to cultivating a good experience for them, and captive customers who fail to have a good customer experience result in unhappy and unengaged customers who have one foot outside the door.

And, you guessed it, captive customers may not be captive forever.

In my opinion, captive customers should receive an even higher level of care and consideration because a once-captive customer could become a now and forever loyal customer. They have expectations primed to be exceeded.

Put Theory Into Practice

Identify Any Captive Customers

Consider all of the ways in which customers may be your captives.

Think about cost, location, product, service and your place in the market, are any of these captivity creators?

Do your research and ask directly why customers are your customers. Don't be afraid of this answer, knowledge is power, as they say.

Enhance the Captive Customer Experience: Work on building a high level of customer satisfaction for captive customers, ensuring that they have a sense of value and of being valued.

Consider the Debt Collection company, which is the most acute form of Captive Customer. These customers could have a really poor experience, resulting in a lack of engagement. A lack of engagement would result in a lack of liability repayment, and an increase in activity from the debt collection company would likely result, such as more contact attempts, more admin, more resources, and more cost.

However, if the experience was optimised and the customer was satisfied, then proactive company contact could be reduced, efficiency would be experienced, and the engaged customer would be more likely to meet their liabilities (pay).

Improve Captive Customer Communication

Captive customers should be well communicated with, communication is your conduit to getting to know each other and building a relationship.

Make the communication relatable and personal, ensuring that you care and value their custom despite any forced nature of the initial relationship (think back to Purdy & Figg's great communication.

Be transparent about any limitations or constraints.

Introduce Perks

What can you offer customers to show that you care? How about a loyalty program where members get perks? Or a discount card? Or a regular newsletter with offers and promotions?

Whatever the perks look like, including benefits or rewards, may mitigate any sense of displeasure that captivity might create. Plus, do you recall what we discussed in the section on loss aversion?

Giving customers something to lose (such as loyalty benefits) can be persuasive in retaining customers.

Innovate and Differentiate

Strive to offer quality and innovation, ensuring that customers choose to stay when they do have a choice.

Ok, so that won't work for debt collection customers, but for the customer who can start to afford to fly with a swankier airline or shop at a more affluent store, and for the garage customer who has a new garage to choose and the displeased earbud-buyer who sought a new bud-brand, perhaps when the time comes, and they have the ability to free themselves, maybe if you offer something enticing, they may just want to stay.

> **I was a drama teacher, so I had the opportunity to show off in front of a captive audience. I essentially did 13 years of stand-up. Whether my pupils would agree that I was remotely interesting or not is another question.**

Greg Davies - Comedian

The 3 S's

Success, Satisfaction and Sentiment

The 3 S's
Success, Satisfaction and Sentiment

What makes a good customer interaction?

We talk constantly about interactions in the world of customer experience, and if you haven't missed it, I have almost religiously banged on in this book about how important it is that these interactions result in some kind of positive emotion. So, what makes a good interaction?

From my years of experience, painstakingly inspecting hundreds, neigh, thousands of experiences, I have deduced that, quite simply, a good interaction comes down to the inclusion of three elements. Success, Satisfaction and Sentiment.

This applies to all industries and all interactions, be they digital or in-person or carried out by a human or artificial intelligence (AI). No matter what your business is, whether it's essential or luxury, I haven't found a scenario where this doesn't work.

Let Me Explain With A Story

I am a customer of an on-demand fitness app called FIIT. It is brilliant, I mean really brilliant. If, like me, you hate repetition, then you will love this app as I am now something like twelve hundred classes deep, and I am still not repeating classes.

And no, before you think it, this isn't a paid ad, I sadly don't get a commission which is a real shame because, boy oh boy, I preach about this company. But back to the story.

I am a customer of FIIT, and I spent a wonderful year smashing through their high-intensity programmes. My subscription ended, and upon renewal, I accidentally subscribed to the monthly subscription rather than the annual one, which, as is usually the case, was the more expensive renewal option.

Now I knew that I could go into Apple settings, cancel the monthly subscription and, next month, renew with the annual subscription as I planned. But that would mean I'd be paying for a year and one month, kind of mitigating some of the savings I'd be making with an annual subscription. I know, I was being a little petty over the money, I guess it's the Yorkshire girl in me, but hey, if you look after the pennies…

Anyway, I thought I'd get in touch with their customer service team and see if they could help a girl out. I'd never used their customer service before (a good sign), so I had no idea what to expect.

I contacted them through live chat, and despite it being around six pm, I received an immediate response from Gemma. I explained what I had mistakenly done, and Gemma responded by telling me what I already knew, that I could cancel and re-subscribe to the annual membership, she even sent me step-by-step instructions on how to do this.

To be honest, I expected this.

I was just taking a punt and was pretty content to receive this answer. I wasn't happy, but I wasn't disappointed either; it was what it was. I was busy cracking on with a different task, and after I'd skimmed through Gemma's message, I just left it there on screen, distracted by something else. I didn't respond.

Eight minutes later, another message from Gemma popped up.

"Alternatively...", Gemma went on to explain that I should follow the instructions she shared, but this time, she gave me a twenty-five percent discount code to apply. This more than covered the cost of the month paid for and resulted in a further discount on the annual membership cost (very happy Yorkshire girl).

As soon as the chat ended, I went online and left Gemma and FIIT a raving review. I was so impressed with the FIIT customer service.

Did you spot the success, satisfaction and sentiment in my story?

I'll break it down.

Put Theory Into Practice

Success

This is a simple requirement for a customer to meet their need or achieve their goal.

Every customer interacts with you for a reason, it might be that they want to buy a product or a service, obtain some information, or perhaps they just want to engage with you on social media.

In my case with FIIT, I, of course, wanted to renew the annual membership.

Now, if I had left the interaction after the first message from Gemma, I would have achieved success because I knew how to change to an annual subscription.

Satisfaction

Satisfaction is achieved in an interaction when the interaction is carried out in a way that meets your customer's needs.

For example, it should be easy to interact with you, perhaps it's quick, anybody the customer speaks to should be confident and knowledgeable, and the customer should be able to interact with you on a channel of their choice (not like the Housing Association scenario I gave where residents were forced to use Whatsapp).

In my example with FIIT, satisfaction was achieved because I was responded to immediately, even though it was 6 p, and I'd considered this possibly out of hours.

Gemma, the agent I spoke with, was responsive, pleasant and helpful. I could use live chat, the channel of my preference, and it was easy and quick to find this contact option.

Once again, if I had left the interaction after the first message from Gemma, I would have achieved satisfaction and would have left the interaction feeling okay and satisfied, but not to the point of advocating.

Sentiment

Here's where the magic happens, as they say.

Sentiment.

Sentiment is an attitude, thought, or judgment prompted by a feeling or an idea and coloured by emotion.*

So, the third element of a successful interaction is the ability to spark a feeling, an emotion within your customer. This isn't just about big or expensive gestures (although have at it

*Dictionary definition, www.merriam-webster.com/dictionary/sentiment

if that's your bag), no, sentiment can be created by showing thought, care and creativity or simply demonstrating personalisation.

Bringing you back one last time to my FIIT experience, Gemma conjured sentiment during our interaction. Firstly, the chat was open at what I considered out of hours.

That created a surprise, a happy surprise (exceeding expectations) that meant I got an instant response rather than a holding message, which I had expected.

Then, completely unprovoked by me, after eight minutes, when most would consider the chat abandoned, Gemma returned to me with an even better solution.

It was like she really understood what I was asking, it wasn't about the membership change, it was about the money, and although I didn't express that explicitly to her, it was like she knew, and in those eight minutes she thought, "I can do better", and she did.

This made me exceptionally happy, not just because of the discount she gave but because, once again, I was genuinely very surprised by the second message, it really felt like she thought about me and cared, I was a person, not just a number.

That sentiment, those happy feelings flowing through me, is what nudged me into Promotor Mode, and I actively went online to leave a review, the ultimate action we would all love our customers to do.

It is important to note that a customer can achieve 'success' without being satisfied. For example, your customer might successfully buy your product, but the website might be a nightmare to navigate, or the shop assistant may be bored and rude. The customer would have achieved their goal (product bought), but they might not have been satisfied with the experience.

Likewise, a customer can be satisfied without achieving success. They may call your customer service to troubleshoot something, and perhaps the troubleshooting isn't successful, and your customer will have to wait for an investigation and a callback.

However, they managed to contact you with ease, Agent Andy was confident and helpful, and your customer understands that more needs to be understood before their goal can be reached.

And you guessed it, sentiment can also be achieved without success. You and Agent Andy might both be huge fans of the Great British Bake Off and whilst troubleshooting, you might enjoy an in-depth analysis of last night's episode where Geoff just walked off the show (shock!). You will leave this interaction feeling like you have made a connection and that Agent Andy cared, and you will remember what a friendly company Agent Andy is to engage with.

Ultimately though, you should aim to achieve all three in every single interaction and success, satisfaction, and sentiment don't happen by accident, they need to intentionally be designed into your experience.

You need to understand what your customers want and what they expect and how to design and empower your team to cultivate sentiment.

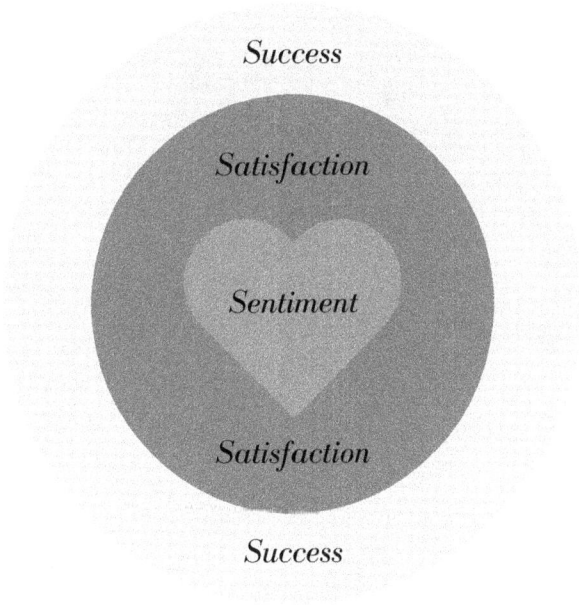

Success

Satisfaction

Sentiment

Satisfaction

Success

Customer Service

Recovery Paradox

Customer Service Recovery Paradox

Oh, I've been excited to write this section!

Please tell me that you are familiar with the **Customer Service Recovery Paradox** and that you use it. No? Well, you soon will.

The Customer Service Recovery Paradox is the concept that a customer can achieve higher levels of satisfaction after the good company management of a bad experience than they would have had if there had been no bad experience at all.

This is amazing because no matter what goes wrong with your customer experience, the recovery paradox presents an opportunity to create even more emotionally engendered customers (emotionally engendered is the right way).

And let's face it, something will always go wrong. It doesn't matter how prepared you are, how customer-centric your policies and procedures are or how brilliant your team are, sometimes things just go wrong. Technology fails, people get sick, and external factors can impact you, but if you are prepared, you can use these failures to nurture a great customer experience.

The Customer Service Recovery Paradox is believed to have this effect for a number of reasons, one being that your customer feels looked after and cared for.

Yes, OK, something has gone wrong, and that isn't great, but we are all customers and, for the most part, can rationalise when something goes wrong. When something goes wrong, and you can demonstrate an intent to fix it and a sincere apology, then your customer is going to feel like you have their best interests in mind, and that you are reliable and can be trusted.

Perceived Justice also plays its part. When a customer feels wronged in some way they naturally want justice to be achieved, for that wrong to be set right and so if you can fix the issue and recover the experience in some way, you are creating that perceived sense of justice for your customer. All is right once again.

As the Head of Customer Experience for Europe's largest Credit Management Company, I had my first real experience with customer experience recovery, and it became a true passion project.

The organisation, like many, had processes that weren't perfect, employees that made mistakes and technology that needed a shake-up. However, unlike most organisations, a bad customer experience could have a significantly negative impact on our customer's circumstances and damage an already 'sensitive' relationship. It was critical to develop a process that enabled us to remedy a negative customer experience quickly; fortunately, the organisation understood this need.

Together we created a process that supported the proactive

identification and customer-centric remedy of high-impacting customer issues, it also supported a much-needed cultural shift by bringing the leaders of multiple departments together to design solutions based on customer needs and wants.

We named this process **ICE, Impacting Customer Events**, I became known as the ICE Queen (a nicer name than it sounds), and ICE was invoked when a customer-impacting event was known.

But customer experience recovery comes in many forms and it doesn't have to be a complex process built to deal with extreme problems, it can come in more simplistic forms, as demonstrated by this next example.

This example comes from Ritz Carlton, world-renowned for its epic customer experience. When I read this example quite some time ago, I couldn't help but smile and start sharing it with anyone who would listen.

While Mrs Customer stayed at a Ritz Carlton resort, she informed a staff member of a plumbing issue in her bathroom. She later dinned in the hotel restaurant, during which time a service team member promptly fixed the issue in her room. Mrs Customer returned not only to find the problem resolved but also to a personal note from the plumber with his name and number on it, asking her to call him directly should the problem occur again. With it, there was a little chocolate wrench.

This isn't rocket science, but it is a brilliant example of how a personal touch and a little creativity can turn a negative experience into one which is guaranteed to make your customer smile. I bet you can think of a few examples you have heard of or even experienced yourself.

It's widely known that it is more profitable to retain an existing customer than to acquire a new one, and equally as important, loyal customers are more likely to be your best asset by telling all of their friends and family about you and recommending you on review sites.

Another benefit not to be ignored is that organisations that excel at providing a great customer experience are likelier to have engaged employees, thus creating the much-coveted cycle of the Employee Experience - Customer Experience Loop (coming up in the next section).

Also, consider the cost you could be avoiding. The cost of handling complaints (especially if you are a regulated industry), the cost of bad press, the cost of bad reviews, the cost of unhappy employees, then the cost of recruitment and the costs of issues identified too late. All of these costs can be mitigated by using effective customer experience recovery.

The bottom line is that customer experience recovery looks very different for every organisation, but as long as you leave your customers feeling happy and satisfied despite any hiccups they face, you are on the right track to remarkable recovery, cost savings, brand enhancement and excellent customer retention.

Put Theory Into Practice

3 Simple Steps For Implementation (ICE).

Plan For Failure

I am not a 'glass half empty' type of person but when it comes to customer experience, it is so important to recognise that no matter how much we care, no matter how much we plan, design and cultivate, sometimes things go wrong.

It pays to try and, where possible, recognise and prepare for these possibilities.

The process you design should:

- **Provide guidance on how to recover from a poor experience:** Where possible, give clear guidance and empower your team, allowing them to react within your set perimeters but still to do so flexibly.

- **Let your team know what they are supported to do:** Be clear on what is and isn't possible, for example, if you have a compensation policy, set clear levels of compensation permitted for each category of issue.

- **Set expectations on how quickly you want the team to act:** Speed is critical, you should aim to proactively identify and remedy a bad experience before your customer has to take any of their own action.

- **Support a collaborative approach across your organisation:** Don't work in silos. An issue that one customer experiences could be an issue many customers experience, so work with your team to fully understand the situation.

- **Promote an issue-tolerant culture:** A hidden problem isn't helpful to anyone, ensure your team is confident in raising issues without fear of repercussion.

- **Close the loop:** Where appropriate, keep your customers informed. You might have only one or two customers who told you about the problem, but you may have many more impacted, so don't be afraid to hold your hands up, acknowledge the problem and proactively apologise, customers appreciate honesty and sincerity.

Empower Employees

Your team is your best asset for a fantastic recovery from a customer experience! If they can quickly spot an issue, speedily remedy it, leave that customer feeling good and prevent a possible complaint, then you have become the master of customer experience recovery.

Empower your team to become' Recovery Heroes' by:

- **Providing them with clear guidance:** Detailed in step one, above.

- **Empower them to act on their authority:** With the proper guidance and support, your team should have the confidence to act quickly using their initiative.

- **Support creativity and personalisation:** Where suitable, promote the use of creative customer experience recovery... Think back to the Ritz Carlton and their handyman sweetening (pun intended) the situation with chocolate wrenches. Creative, personalised solutions will leave a lasting good impression.

Fix The Issue!

You've done it.

You've turned a poor experience into a great experience, and you now have a happy customer! But your work isn't quite finished yet, now comes the part where you do everything possible to prevent any other customer from experiencing the same initial poor experience.

Now is the time to:

- **Identify the root cause of the problem**

- **Understand its impact:** Is it a one-off or a repeating issue? Has it impacted the few or the many?

- **Work with your team to fix the problem:** Collaboration is key. Work with the broader team to ensure the issue is fully identified and fixed

- **Throw in some additional quality assurance to ensure your 'fix' has worked:** Monitor that experience, and map the journey your customers are taking to make sure the experience you intended is now the experience they are getting.

Plan, empower and fix (including prevent) is the key to successfully recovering an experience, gone wrong.

> **" Making a mistake provides an opportunity to show the lengths you will go to, to fix it "**

Katie Stabler - CX-er

The
EX-CX
Loop

The EX-CX Loop

This book is about customer experience, but you will likely have heard lots of different 'experience' terms in the world of business.

The **Human** Experience, **Total** Experience, **User** Experience, **Guest** Experience and, of course, **Employee** Experience (feel free to add more to the list).

These terms are not to be ignored; experiences are all connected and some are so nuanced they require explicit attention. But my stance is that there is a lot to do in all areas, and one can not stretch oneself too thinly and dilute the effect you have, so I have very firmly planted myself in the world of customer experience.

I can not exclude this small section on the Employee Experience (EX) - Customer Experience (CX) Loop because it sets the foundations for cultural change and helps explain why employee experience and customer experience are so interlinked.

I use this regularly within my training to help employees understand just how valuable customer experience is to them and how they are to customer experience.

The EX-CX Loop

- The EX-CX Loop is the simple idea that the employee does a good job, is confident, expert, and friendly, and delivers a good customer experience.

- The customer recognises the good customer experience they have received and feels satisfied, perhaps even happy, about the interaction.

- The customer makes an effort to leave the employee great feedback.

- The employee sees this feedback and revels in their great job.

- The feeling of happiness buoys the employees, and they work at optimum efficiency, following processes, adhering to policy, returning from breaks on time, etc. They put in extra effort with the next customer to make them as satisfied as the last.

- Thus, the virtuous cycle continues in a loop.

It's a simple theory, but gosh, it makes sense.

Whilst this is a theory, it is supported by a considerable volume of research and anecdotal evidence. Let's look at the research first.

Research

Gallup's "State of the American Workplace" survey (2014) produced a report to support organisations in nurturing a more highly engaged workforce, as a staggering amount of revenue is lost through passively or actively unengaged employees.

Perhaps unsurprisingly, they found that organisations with more engaged employees were simply more profitable and that engagement has a more significant impact on an employee than corporate policies and perks (and interestingly, they found that women tend to be more engaged workers).

Organisations with engaged employees experience a whopping 240% boost in performance-related business outcomes compared to organisations with less engaged employees.

So, if employee engagement is so crucial, what drives engagement? Well, there are many factors, as you might imagine. Having the right manager is essential, as is using realistic goals and measures and the ability to connect with your employees. But guess what they also found. Customer experience is also crucial to employee engagement. They report, "Optimising the emotional connection between employees and customers must be central to what leaders and managers think about every day." (There's that word again, emotion).

Coming a little closer to our current timeline, a decade later, in 2022, The Harvard Business Review (HBR) put a microscope over years of employee and financial data from a global retailer. It produced a report from their research: **How Employee Experience Impacts Your Bottom Line.**

The researchers recognised the claims that employee experience has a causal effect on customer experience and the financial impact of a customer experience on the business. However, despite the claims, the evidence to demonstrate that causal effect was thin. So, they set out to find unequivocal evidence to prove this link and show company leaders the ROI within the investment of their employees and customer experience.

They succeeded! They found undeniable evidence of the link between employee experience and revenue, gob-smacking proof, actually. They could show that if a store could move their employees from the bottom quartile to the top quartile within each employee experience metric they used, the store would see revenue increase by 50% and a profit increase by almost that much. They summarised (and I love this statement) that, "Any organisation that has customer-facing employees should realise that they matter immensely to business success. They are not simply a cost to be minimised - as retail, call centre and service employees are far too often thought of by executives - but potentially very high impact investments.".

Well said HBR, a round of applause. Although they call out customer-facing employees here, they do recognise in the report that all employees have an impact on customer experience, but of course, customer-facing employees are the catalyst in how your customer experience is translated to your customers.

This point is so important right now. In our world of fast-developing artificial intelligence (AI), many companies are trying to do more with less, which often comes from human resource efficiencies. We must ask ourselves, how well can we succeed in creating an emotional connection with our customers if we use humans less and less?

Ok, I have one more piece of research to share with you. A year later, in 2023, Deloitte shared that an empowered workforce increases brand engagement and customer loyalty. We are becoming a little more nuanced here. Although engagement will come into it, in this research, Deloitte has honed in on employee empowerment (a crucial feature of a happy employee and essential to strategies like the 3 S's and the Customer Service Recovery Paradox). Deloitte found that workers with excellent employee experience were three times more likely to say their organisation is customer-focused and one point five times more likely to enjoy working directly with their customers and clients. So, Deloitte has identified a striking result of organisational customer focus impacting the employee experience.

Anecdotal Evidence

The research is one thing, but you might be reading this thinking, 'Show me it in practice; give me examples where we can see this working, please'.

I can. Fear not.

Over the last three years, Samsung Electronics (2021) and Microsoft (2022 and 2023) have won Forbes' top hundred best workplaces. Employees vote for these companies and call them great places to work. Staff also vote for accolades; both Samsung and Microsoft can boast a lot of recognition regarding customer experience.

Samsung can be seen at regular customer experience awards, including winning the Best Innovation in Customer Experience (2022) and Best Brand Experience (2023). They also ranked highly in the 2022 American Customer Service Index (ACSI), one of the most robust and long-standing customer service reports you can find (established in 1994, with the UKCSI following quite sometime later in 2008). This doesn't scratch the surface of Samsung CX's claims.

Microsoft, like Samsung flirts heavily with customer experience recognition. Around the time of reaching the top of the Forbes list, they saw a spike in customer satisfaction, sitting at 79/100 on the ACSI.

But let's not ignore the rest of the Forbes list; the top spot is excellent, but getting within the top ten rankings is something to be proud of, too. And guess who we see sitting at number eight on the Forbes list of the top one hundred places to work? IKEA! Yes. If you recall the anecdote shared about IKEA in the Peak End Rule Section, are we surprised to see them also recognised for excellent employee experience?

Placed just beneath IKEA is Lego, at number nine. Lego is synonymous with customer service, priding itself in its responsive and personalised customer service.

There's a vast library of excellent customer service stories I could share from Lego, but the story of Luka Apps tugged at my customer experience heartstrings; Seven-year-old Luka lost his favourite Ninjago figure during a shopping trip, Jay ZX (yeah, I have no idea who this either but if you Google him he's a pretty scary looking dude in blue). Luka wrote to LEGO to tell them and wait for it, promising to take better care if a replacement was provided (heart melt). In response, LEGO's customer service representative, Richard, wrote to Luka that he had consulted with Sensei Wu (a character from Ninjago), who approved sending a new Jay ZX figure along with an additional "bad guy" for Jay to fight. Richard also ingeniously included some advice from Sensei Wu, which expressed that Luka really should take great care of his Lego.

As I said, this fantastic response is just one of many. Put yourself in Richards's shoes. How could you not be happy and engaged working at Lego? You are empowered to be creative and make your customers' day, so it is no wonder that Lego is featured in Forbes' top 100 workplaces. It is the EX-CX Loop at its best.

Employee and customer experience are intrinsically linked; you can't have one without another. Research shows that companies that understand this and act on it will reap the most benefits from investing in their employees and customers (more on this in the section focused on culture).

*Lego story courtesy of BrickView Youtube channel: Lego Customer Services Stories

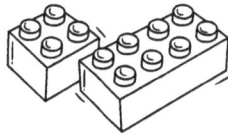

Expectations
vs
Performance

Expectations VS Performance

I should probably touch on an essential clarification at this point.

Throughout this book, I have discussed and will continue to discuss **customer experience**. Yes, I have referenced customer service, and I have spoken of employees and total experience; there are many titles, names, and buzzwords that float around in the business world.

Commonly, there are three very well-known headliners: customer service, customer experience and customer success. Quite honestly, although each of these is relatively well understood, companies tend to have their own definitions of each, with their own nuance, which vary between industry and country. So we are all on the same page, my definition of these three are as follows:

Customer service is a support function that businesses implement to directly manage and support customer interactions such as enquiries, feedback, and complaints. It can consist of self-service features, artificial intelligence support (like chatbots), and human resources: people to talk to when customers need something.

Customer success is a relationship management and sales function. Typically, customer success departments and roles are seen in business-to-business (B2B) environments.

They have evolved to ensure that a customer relationship is well-managed and nurtured and that customers use the products or services effectively to reach the expected outcome. These roles ensure that customer needs are met and that innovation and development are shared with the customer, encouraging the relationship's growth. Customer success is often connected to sales and business growth.

Customer experience is a movement. OK, some of you might not recognise it or think of it as a movement, although I hope you do by the end of this book. In its more traditionally known definition, customer experience is the design and management of every interaction your customer has with you. From the first moment they become aware of you to when they say goodbye, customer experience encompasses everything. Customer service and success are nestled within and part of the customer experience.

I am highlighting these definitions now because when discussing customer expectations, it is essential to recognise what creates and influences them and how the performance of customer service and customer success (and many other departments, such as marketing, finance, and sales) can lead to high or low customer satisfaction.

Where Is The Expectation Seed Planted?

Unsurprisingly, expectations are cultivated from the first moment a customer becomes aware of you. This can occur in one of three ways.

Customers may hear about you from a friend, family member, or someone in their professional network.

They might hear about you via your marketing and advertising.

Or they may hear about you from a third-party source, like a news, review or comparison site.

Either way, all three of these awareness avenues could create a positive or negative expectation. Someone might mention you for good or bad reasons, and your advertising might or might not resonate with them. News, reviews, or comparison sites could share good news and reviews or bad news and reviews, and you could be at the top or bottom of the comparison list.

If, from day one, customers are seeing and hearing less than positive things about you, then let's face it, they are probably rather unlikely to become your customers. That is, of course, unless they are a sucker for punishment, loss aversion doesn't apply to them, or they really, really want what only you can offer (captive!). So, for this section, we will pop these customers aside and work on the notion that, actually, from day one, these customers are seeing and hearing positive things, and they proceed to become your customers.

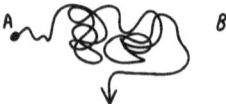

Seed Rot Or Flower Growth?

We are talking about customer expectations vs business performance, so the first thing to ask is: Are the positive expectations set by your customers' first awareness of you being met?

This is where I like to think of marketing and sales as your promise to the customer, and your customer experience is how you actually deliver on this promise. This is, unfortunately, where companies can fall at the first hurdle, where you over-promise and under-deliver, or just promise and don't deliver, where the customer expectations go unmet (consider the example I shared when focusing on loss aversion, the B2B subscription I purchased, which did not meet my expectations at all).

Customers create expectations based on their own history, experience, and bias. They build on this with the messages you share, the images you create, and the perceptions you try to design. You might be great at cultivating those perceptions, so great that customers buy. But are you great at delivering what you promised? If you're not, then yes, you guessed it, loss aversion will hit. Your customer will, of course, feel dissatisfied, resulting from a feeling of loss (money/trust).

What's Behind An Unmet Expectation?

Let's explore unmet expectations more deeply by introducing mental models and the Cognitive Appraisal Theory.

We humans like to make things easy for ourselves, and one way that we do this—or should I say that our brains do this? We use cognitive frameworks called mental models. A mental model helps us do many things, including solving problems and making decisions.

The most applicable mental model to this topic is that it allows us to predict outcomes. Mental models are cultivated by what we see, experience, and believe.

In the case of unmet expectations, the gap and ultimate feeling of dissatisfaction occurs when our mental model is challenged (our brains do not like this) when the actual outcome differs from the expected outcome. How intensely we react to that difference in expectation is decided by our view of the situation and our cognitive appraisal.

The Cognitive Appraisal Theory was developed in the 1980s by psychologists Richard Lazarus and Susan Folkman. The theory explains how our emotions are triggered by our evaluation of a situation, not the actual situation itself.

This is incredibly valuable to know as it can explain why customers sometimes act in what seems like an irrationally heightened way to a scenario that doesn't seem to warrant such a reaction. They have gone through a cognitive appraisal and determined that, at that moment, the situation feels like it has impacted their well-being somehow, and their interpretation of the situation warrants their reaction.

I don't know about you, but I have been there. I'm sorry to say I have been that irrational customer.

I recall a minor issue I had recently in which I was ordering some next-day printing from a company I regularly use, and they paused my order due to a printing design discrepancy.

I was ordering an item intended for portrait use, yet I uploaded a landscape design. I knew what I was doing; I had done this many times before, and despite the oddity of the order, it was accurate.

Irrespective of my doing this repeatedly, they still paused the order to check this was accurate before committing to print. Granted, their process is sensible, and in the light of a new day, I can see reason, but at that moment, clearly panicked by an urgent order being postponed, my cognitive appraisal process told me that this issue was significantly impacting and warranted worry, upset and anger.

Loss aversion likely kicked in, and I lost my perceived control. With stabby fingers, I heavily typed out irksome and short-tempered responses to a customer care agent who was only trying to assist (I was never sweary, rude, mean or personal, I have to say. I just wasn't my usual amenable self and for that, I have a sprinkle of personal shame).

In these scenarios, we go through two levels of appraisal: primary and secondary. It happens quickly, and we are not subconsciously aware of it.

During the primary appraisal, we determine if the mismatch is good or bad or doesn't really have an impact either way.

In my printing example, my unmet expectation of the order being processed smoothly (from my reaction) was clearly appraised as bad and impacting my goal.

However, the next time it happens, I'd like to think that with my growing knowledge and added context to the situation, my cognitive appraisal would recognise it as neutral, knowing that a simple confirmation will progress the order.

If the primary appraisal doesn't think the situation is significant, then the cognitive appraisal clocks off until the following appraisal scenario comes along.

But, if the situation is considered important (impacting), then the secondary appraisal occurs. Within this appraisal, our brains evaluate the situation further, considering whether we can influence it and if we are equipped to deal with it.

We then think ahead to the possible consequences that might impact us, and the worse we feel about these, the more frustrated, upset, or angry we will likely become. (This also occurs when an unexpected positive consequence is likely; here, we would experience more preferable emotions such as happiness, excitement and joy).

Again, using my printing example, I believe I could have influenced the situation and had the capability to do so, hence my frustrated conversation with the customer care agent. It's easy to identify the negative consequences I created worry over. I must have had a concern that my next-day delivery requirement wouldn't be fulfilled, which led to worry, which flowed out of me as frustration and anger.

Unmet expectations are much more complex than we see at face value. There is so much behind how expectations come to be and what makes us decide, subconsciously or consciously, if they have been met.

Organisations that understand this can then equip themselves to set and successfully manage expectations at any point in the customer experience life cycle. Cognitive appraisal theory provides a fascinating view of how customers evaluate experiences based on their expectations, emotions, and perceived outcomes.

Put Theory Into Practice

Understand Your Customer Expectations And How They Have Been Cultivated

All of the data points at your disposal (Voice of the customer, sentiment analysis, the voice of your employee, behavioural data, etc..) to understand what your customer expectations actually are.

Don't make assumptions here; their expectations may not be what you think.

Following this, you need to understand what cultivates that expectation. Is it brand perception? Is it a message in your marketing? Is it previous use? What actually manipulates how a customer thinks and feels about you?

It's also a worthwhile exercise to ensure you know your customer's goals and, subsequently, if the outcome you provide achieves their goal. If it doesn't, there's a big, unmet expectation right there.

It might sound strange, but your customer's goal may not be as apparent as it seems; for example, a customer purchasing a flight (in most cases) doesn't have the goal to fly. Their goal is to reach a destination safely. This more profound understanding of customer goals is known as the Jobs To Be Done Framework; it was popularised in 2003 by Clayton M. Christensen, a renowned professor at Harvard Business School, in collaboration with his colleagues, particularly Anthony W. Ulwick and later Bob Moesta. There's a section dedicated to this next, so I'll say no more about this just now.

Design Emotional Triggers Into Your Experience

What? Are we talking about emotion again? YES! Of course, we are. Emotion is vital in CX, and I will continue to reiterate that throughout the book because it is really that important.

Cognitive Appraisal Theory joins our cognitive appraisal with our emotional reactions and offers reasons as to why we behave as we do. This is valuable to creating customer satisfaction and is a reason why customers choose to be our customers.

Specifically (and expertly), designing emotional triggers for your experience at crucial points can effectively support expectations being met or exceeded.

To do this, you need to execute step one above and understand your customer expectations and how they have been cultivated.

Using this insight alongside a spot of customer journey mapping, you can pinpoint crucial moments of the customer experience, often called the Moments That Matter, to identify where the most positively triggered emotions will drive the most significant impact.

It could be onboarding, the point of sales or problem resolution; it will be different for each business and industry (and even customer persona), and so you need to use data and insight (and even trial and error) to find those most emotionally evocative points. I would start with where the most complaints are and where the most positive feedback is targeted.

Whilst these areas shouldn't be relied upon alone (there is so much to be found in what goes unsaid: refer back to the 'Listen to the layers of meaning' section), if you are stuck for where to start, these are a good bet. Customers are emotionally triggered at these points, so much so that they are willing to go out of their way to either complain or leave feedback, so they should be recognised as essential and triggering parts of the customer journey.

Don't Skip A Beat

Monitor real-time feedback and identify, at the moment, what causes emotional responses and don't stop there; react to them.

Previously, we would need to rely on direct customer feedback to provide this insight. But now we have the benefit of conversational analytics and sentiment analysis to monitor emotion, and whilst I don't believe AI is the be-all and end-all in CX, there are some use cases (such as this) that I strongly advocate that all businesses use.

Seriously, if you don't, you are behind and missing so much. This kind of real-time data can enable us to act in the moment and improve a customer's experience. It can also alter the broader operations (e.g. when recognising a problem that can or does impact multiple customers from just a few customer comments).

Equip Your People

Alongside AI use and employee training, there must be a layer of empowerment. What good is recognising emotional triggers and their impact if your team is powerless to change things for the better? You must allow a degree of flexibility and freedom, ensuring your team can ultimately do the right thing (and if you recall, this act of empowerment goes a long way in driving the EX-CX loop).

Recognise Change

The one constant is change.

You have probably heard that before, and I hope it rings true. Everything in the business world constantly changes, and your customers aren't immune to that change.

Their expectations are subject to change for many reasons, so in point one of this section, I recommend that you understand your customer expectations and how you have cultivated them. Of course, it's essential to keep reviewing this to ensure you are meeting them.

I'll share another anecdote here, erm, with a somewhat embarrassing end, but embarrassment is the price I am willing to pay to ensure you can optimise your customer experience.

I have had the pleasure of flying business class many times (and first class just once). I flew business class with a particular, well-known airline several times. While their business class cabin wasn't the best I'd experienced, it had always been a good flight with excellent cabin crew and all the usual bells and whistles. Overall, it was a positive, memorable experience, and my expectations were set.

A few years passed, and the opportunity to fly with them arose again. I decided to splurge and upgrade my seat at the last minute, and wow, I was sorely disappointed.

The business class cabin, whilst I recalled it was not the best out of all the airlines I have experienced, seemed smaller and tired. The previously excellent, super friendly, bend-over-backwards cabin crew were far from that on this occasion. I'd actually go as far as saying one member of the crew was really rude and made me feel embarrassed when ordering a drink. And finally, the on-flight bar, which I was really looking forward to enjoying, was out of order.

(It was considered usable by the crew, which really was a joke considering the lights were broken, and unless you were a fan of sitting in the dark, it was absolutely not usable!).

While at the point of booking the flight, my expectations had not changed, the experience of the subpar flight resulted in an expectation change.

Although the experience was not terrible enough for me to decide that I would never fly with this airline again, I did vow never to waste money on their business class again because my expectations had gone unmet, leading to new, low expectations.

Yet, fate would decide otherwise…

I accidentally upgraded to business class for the return flight home (insert facepalm here or a Homer Simpson esk 'doh'!).

Yes, it did occur to me that I might be the only person daft enough to do that; I told you this story was embarrassing.

When I tried to reverse the mistaken transaction, the customer care agent basically told me, 'The computer says no. ' I was devastated. This expense was unbudgeted, and after such a poor experience on the last flight, I hated the thought of spending more money on a repeat.

Thankfully, the airline gods took pity on my self-induced plight and saved me, and the return flight offered a completely different, epic experience.

The airline lounge in New York, JFK, was considerably better than in Manchester. The plane was new, and the cabin was FANTASTIC; it was bigger and more modern. It had increased functionality and completely closable private cabins for total comfort and privacy, and it rivalled some of the more luxurious airlines I'd travelled with.

Lastly, the cabin crew was like how I'd initially remembered them: excellent, super friendly, and would bend backwards to make your trip outstanding.

This secondary experience once again changed my expectations. Despite deciding that I'd never upgrade with this airline again, after just a couple of weeks and a significantly better experience, my expectations had grown tenfold. They were much higher than they had been in the first place (a little dot of customer service recovery can be spotted here).

So, do you see what I mean when I say you need to keep up to date with your customer's expectations? My ridiculous story of quickly altered customer expectations might feel extreme, but it isn't that unusual.

Think of the customer who had a poor experience with you but then became converted by a friend who raved positively about you. Or consider the customer who loves and has been loyal to you but decides to leave after a particularly irksome experience. Expectations can change easily and quickly.

Be More

Bridge

Be More Bridge
(The Halo Effect Theory)

If only you could be a bridge.

Not any bridge. The Brooklyn Bridge.

And not you per se, but your business.

If only your business could be the Brooklyn Bridge!!!

What am I talking about??? Let me explain.

I have now visited Brooklyn Bridge (the bridge joining Manhattan and Brooklyn) for the 3rd time. The last time I visited, it was baltic and walking the one point one mile from Brooklyn to Manhattan in gusty, freezing winds didn't present the ideal walking climate.

I was thoroughly wrapped up, layered with thermals and decorated with a hat, gloves and a scarf, yet the cold still penetrated and nibbled at me painfully. But I smiled, walked, saw the stunning sights and enjoyed every second.

The Brooklyn Bridge is one of those places that guarantees a great experience, no matter the imperfections. As a visitor walking its path, you don't care about the weather, the significant drop below visible through the lats (honestly, don't look down), or the hoards of people that crowd the path, taking selfies.

You don't care about this because places like the Brooklyn Bridge evoke positive emotion. It's an icon we have become familiar with growing up through movies (such as The Amazing Spider-Man, Once Upon A Time In America, Fantastic Four and I Am Legend, to name a few); it's a place people talk about; it's something we kind of fall in love with before we ever set our own eyes on it.

Our perception of it is so strong that no matter the imperfections (like the cold and the crowds), we forgive them and enjoy the experience.

This almost unwavering positive view can be related to the Halo Effect Theory.

The Halo Effect Theory is a cognitive bias (yes, another; we really are somewhat biased as a species) which results in our perception of objects, situations, people, and brands being influenced by our overall impression of them. If we have a positive impression, irrespective of facts, evidence or occurrence, then we assume and feel like other elements are positive.

So, in the case of the Brooklyn Bridge, my impression is overwhelmingly positive, and so, despite the less-than-perfect experience I had on my last visit, my positive perception remained intact.

Psychologist Edward Thorndike first coined the term in the 1920s after observing that people rated individuals they liked higher across a range of unrelated attributes. I suppose this is quite a critical bias regarding friends and family, where there might be a need to forgive the occasional misgiving.

Now, can you imagine if your company and your brand created the same effect?

Well, the Halo Effect Theory doesn't just apply to bridges, friends, and family. It, of course, also applies to business.

Branding And Marketing

The Halo Effect Theory is prominent in branding and marketing. Consider the likes of Starbucks; it is such a well-known brand that it serves 14.3 million customers daily (2022 data).

Why? Is it because their coffee is better than that of the local coffee shop down the road? Is it because their service is better? Is it because their cafe is lovelier?

In some cases, evidently, the answer to those questions may all be 'Yes'. But it's undeniable that their prominent branding has created a positive and reliable impression on consumers, which will have created a cognitive bias, leading them to answer yes to one or more of the questions above, even if the coffee, service or atmosphere is not better.

Service

The apparent reference here is Amazon, right? With next-day delivery on almost everything, even same-day delivery in some cases and their pretty decent, no quibble, service return process, Amazon is known for the service it offers customers.

But think about it for a second: is Amazon always cheaper? Does it offer the brand you might prefer? Do more and more other retailers not offer next-day delivery and significant return policies?

Just like with Starbucks, Amazon likely benefits from the Halo Effect, with 12 million of us (I included) every day almost robotically heading to Amazon as the first port of call.

Customer Experience

Whilst I advocate that almost every part of the business sits under this bucket (including the above mention of branding, marketing and service), there are some examples of overt customer experience in which the Halo Effect can be found.

I'll use the Ritz-Carlton as an example; the hotel brand is known for its outstanding approach to customer care. There are endless stories shared across the internet showing the lengths employees go to to make a customer happy, including that of Joshie, the giraffe (oh go on then, I'll give you a quick story summary.

Basically, a small child left their favourite stuffed animal, Joshie the giraffe, at the hotel. Seeing their heartbroken child, the parents called the hotel to ask if Joshie could be found.

Not only was Joshie found, but the staff took photos of Joshie around the hotel, packed him up with the photos, a personalised hotel pass and a letter to the child explaining that Joshie had just decided to extend his holiday!

Come on. How adorable.). Granted, the Ritz-Carlton are really up there when it comes to customer experience (and perhaps for the price tag, they should be), but do customers overlook the occasional grumpy staff member, failed key card, slow drinks order and high price tag because of the overwhelmingly positive impression already cultivated?

I hope you can see that the Halo Effect can be a powerful business tool. If harnessed, it can be significant, especially when things don't always go perfectly.

Put Theory Into Practice

Invest In Emotions

Emotion; the most commonly found word in this book?

Yes, and for good reason.

Regarding the Halo Effect Theory, investing in emotional

branding and experience design is paramount. You aim to develop such an overwhelmingly positive impression that customers will forgive perceived imperfections (to a degree, there is a limit to what customers will and won't permit, even with the presence of the halo effect). To cultivate that positive impression, you need to engender sentiment; customers need to feel something for you, at least a strong fondness.

Design Your Customers' First Impressions

First impressions matter so much, and I will throw another cognitive bias at you here, the primacy effect. It explains how the information we initially take on heavily influences our overall impression.

For example, if we walk into a restaurant, hear a great tune and experience a warm, expert greeting, we are more likely to forgive a minor issue later, such as a delay in our order or a missing side dish.

Build A Strong Identity

The one thing that the examples I have used in this section have in common is that they all have a strong identity, which has all, of course, been built over time with investment and consistency.

While we may not all achieve the brand identity heights that Starbucks, Amazon, and Ritz-Carlton have, we can achieve strong identities that resonate with our target audience.

To do this (aside from strong marketing), highlight your strengths, be that your products, services, customer care or even social responsibility.

Be consistent, too; you can only become well-known for something if you consistently deliver and plaster that perception to the wall of your customer's brains (and hearts).

Know That The Halo Effect Has A Dark Side

Whilst I have focused on the enormous benefits the Halo Effect can have on a business, it is key to understand that it also works the other way around.

We will all aim to nurture that overall positive impression, which leads to customers considering us positively in most areas, even if that isn't quite their experience, but if the overall impression is harmful, even if we excel in some areas, customers may be so cognitively biased that they don't recognise our strengths.

And, as I expressed earlier, this isn't a silver bullet. Whilst the Halo Effect can lead to a widespread perception and a level of forgiveness of an occasional imperfect experience, it will not give you a free pass forever; customers aren't stupid or glutens for punishment.

If only your business could be the Brooklyn Bridge!!!

We should all be more bridge.

Jobs

To Be Done

Jobs To Be Done

If you were paying attention in an earlier section, you would have spotted a mention of this already, but to recap for anyone who may have been snoozing, daydreaming or distracted by your day job/children/pets: The Jobs To Be Done Framework was popularised in 2003 by Clayton M. Christensen, a renowned professor at Harvard Business School, in collaboration with his colleagues, particularly Anthony W. Ulwick and later Bob Moesta.

It's really more well-known in the marketing world (so if you are a marketeer, hi, enjoy.) but is hugely relevant in customer experience (and equally, hugely underused).

It is the ideology of understanding customer goals on a more profound level that, once known, helps you to then meet these goals. Prof Christensen and the team promote the notion that customers 'hire' a product or service to do a job, and once you understand what that job is, you understand the customer's goal.

To explain, I gave this example: a customer purchasing a flight (in most cases) doesn't have the goal to fly. Their goal is to reach a destination safely. Prof Christensen, however, explains the ideology with the pretty well-known milkshake example (There's a YouTube video with over 430,000 watches; I'll share the link below*).

*Professor Christensens Milkshake example: https://www.youtube.com/watch?v=sfGtw2C95Ms

He tells how his team consulted with a well-known fast-food chain that wanted to increase its milkshake sales. During the project, they undertook customer research to find out what motivates a customer to buy a milkshake in the first place. What do you think they discovered? Were customers driven to buy a milkshake from this fast-food chain because:

- The taste was unrivalled?
- The flavour choices were plentiful?
- Was the value unbeaten?
- They just preferred a milkshake over a soda?
- Milkshakes gave them nostalgia for their childhood?

Nope, it was none of the above. What he and his team actually discovered is that the peak in milkshake sales was during the morning commute, before 8 am (milkshake for breakfast, anyone?), and the primary motivator of customers already buying milkshakes was, interestingly, to have something to do on a boring commute to work with the secondary motivator of keeping the tummy satisfied until lunch.

The Job To Be Done here is primarily to cure boredom and, secondarily, to keep them satiated.

Okay, but why a milkshake, I hear you ask?

Well, to help figure this out, they went on to ask customers what other products they 'hired' to do the job (of curing boredom and satiating until lunch), and they heard examples like hiring a banana, but it was gone too quickly, required more than one hand to peel and left them feeling hungry sooner rather than later.

Then there was an example of hiring a bagel, but ultimately, that was deemed too messy and awkward whilst driving.

I was so curious about this when I first came across Jobs To Be Done several years ago. The notion that a product competitor wasn't just another brand but actually entirely different products was a curiosity indeed.

The milkshake was deemed best for the job because a customer could easily hold it with one hand, it was thick and viscous enough that it couldn't be drunk quickly, and it was filling enough to eliminate hunger until lunchtime.

Understanding this motivator, knowing the customer's Job/s To Be Done (goal) results in being able to market the product better and crucial to customer experience, knowing how to improve the product (in this case, maybe the milkshake needs to be even thicker so it takes longer to drink, maybe a dense, healthy smoothie would be a better seller, or perhaps it could be sold with a reusable cup and a reward card so customers feel added value, or even with a cup jacket to keep the customer's hand warm and the milkshake cool during the drive…you get the idea).

Job Dimensions

Understanding the customer's jobs to be done is the first step and the high-level approach to this methodology, but if you progress to considering the three job dimensions, you can take it to the next level, a deeper level of understanding.

The three job dimensions are functional, emotional, and social jobs, and each Job To Be Done can have various dimensions.

Job: This is the core task or goal that a customer wants to accomplish.

Functional Jobs: The practical or utilitarian tasks customers need to accomplish.

Emotional Jobs: The feelings customers seek when using or interacting with the product or service.

Social Jobs: How customers want to be perceived by others or how they relate socially

I used this methodology when designing customer personas with an Airport client, and to help workshop attendees further contextualise those jobs (creating a tangible understanding), I provided these examples:

Job: This is the core task or goal that a customer wants to accomplish. *For example, when an airport passenger buys a sandwich in the cafe, their job is not simply to*

own a sandwich; instead, it's to stop hunger, cure boredom, enable the medication to be taken, keep the children entertained, etc.

Functional Jobs: The practical or utilitarian tasks customers need to accomplish *(e.g., finding a place to sit, getting through security, getting through check-in or dropping off a bag)*

Emotional Jobs: The feelings customers seek when using or interacting with the product or service. *(e.g., feeling safe, comfortable, happy or excited).*

Social Jobs: How customers want to be perceived by others or how they relate socially *(e.g., sitting with a laptop to demonstrate they are on a business trip, wearing designer brands to exude luxury or being assisted and wanting it to be discreet to maintain a perception of being physically able).*

Going one step further, you can consider **Influencers**. Nope, not the type of influence that gets paid an eye-watering sum of money to make TikTok videos (I'm just jealous), this type of influencer:

Influencers: The circumstances under which customers must complete a 'job' influence how they approach it. Again, using the airport as an example, this could include the time of day the travel takes place, delays, and the reason for travel. Commuting by plane weekly has different demands than leisurely, occasional weekend travel.

By identifying why your customer hires your product or service, you can innovate with the knowledge of the needs they require a meeting. You can market better, tuning into their real motivators to buy, and you can ensure there is no expectation gap between wants, needs and reality…you can use this methodology to improve the customer experience in many ways.

Put Theory Into Practice

Identify The Job To Be Done (JTBD)

How you do this depends on where you are in the journey and what customer data and insight you have available. You can take a light-touch approach if you have limited insight and limited resources (like the time and money to conduct analysis and research).

This would rely on an internal review of what you and your employees consider your customer motivations to be. Whilst this is an inside-out view and wouldn't be the most robust approach (because your internal thoughts and feelings can be biased), it can offer a starting point and be incredibly insightful to reframe how you look at customer motivators.

If you are a little more mature in your approach and/or have resources, you can either lean into existing customer insight to help you understand customer motivators or conduct proactive research.

Here, you can interview or observe your customers to understand their motivations, much like Prof Christensen did for the fast food chain. The focus should be to look beyond the product or service and instead focus on the customer's desired outcome. After all, this is about the customers' Job to Be Done and why they 'hire' your product or service rather than the product or service.

Identify The Three Job Dimensions

As highlighted already, after you understand the main Job To Be done, you can grow a deeper level of understanding if you progress to consider the three possible job dimensions.

The three job dimensions are functional, emotional, and social jobs, and each Job To Be Done can have various dimensions.

Use insight to identify which job dimension your customer is trying to achieve.

Figure Out If There Are Any Influencers

Consider what circumstances the customer carries out their job within and if they affect how the customer achieves their job.

Consider time constraints, environmental factors, people factors and emotional states that may shape their wants and decisions.

For example, in the airport scenario, a delayed flight influences how passengers interact with food options (they need a more substantial meal than planned), and their seating choices may be impacted (they need a comfier place to rest than a bar stool).

Look For The Gaps

Now that you know what jobs your customer hires your product or service to do, review your product or service to identify which of these requirements it successfully fulfils clearly.

This activity will enable you to map out what goals you achieve for your customers and, most importantly, what goals (JTBD) you don't.

Ensure that the job dimensions and influencers are included within this analysis to see where gaps or opportunities for innovation exist.

Redefine Your Competitors

As I already mentioned, I became really interested in the idea that your competitors may be much broader than you initially considered, and the JTBD analysis can expand your understanding of who and what a competitor is.

Use this deeper insight to broaden your perspective on competition. Ask: "What else could my customers hire for this job?" Analyse indirect competitors (e.g., milkshakes vs. bananas) to uncover your customers' unmet needs.

Innovate For Improved Experiences (And Sales)

It's all good to grow your insight, but it can't stop there; you need to use that insight to develop your offering to meet your customer's needs better.

For example, If customers hire your product to meet a social need like upgrading to a business class flight to show an air of prestige, consider how you can provide a more visible premium offering to expand how you fulfil their social motivators.

Or if a customer's job is functional and connected to convenience, say they just want a quick meal conveniently located at their place of work. You should consider increasing that convenience, such as offering a pre-order and collection service or even a delivery service.

Embed And Repeat

Like much of what is included within this book, Jobs To Be Done is not a one-time activity.

You change, your employees change, your customers will absolutely change, and as such, your products and services should change (perhaps not wholly, but they should at least evolve).

The principles and methodology we discuss should be well understood within your organisation and become standardised, an embedded process, and a constant part of your business practice. That's the only way to make customer experience a movement, not simply an 'add-on'.

Train your team to adopt the JTBD mindset in every decision, from marketing and product design to customer service and support.

Use workshops or team discussions to practice identifying jobs and brainstorming solutions.

Apply JTBD across the entire customer journey. For example:

- **Pre-sales:** What motivates customers to consider your products and/or services in the first place?

- **Purchase:** What do they need to feel sure about their decision?

- **Post-purchase:** What do they expect to achieve after using the product or service? What engagement do they need?

By following these steps, you can transform the JTBD framework from an abstract concept into a practical tool that drives innovation, improves customer experience, and aligns your business offerings with what truly matters to your customers.

Companies derive significant value from this unique approach to understanding customer goals/wants/needs.

While it can take a second for people to grasp, this enhanced perspective is easy to implement once you start.

Customer Journey Mapping

Customer Journey Mapping (And Management)

Customer Journey Mapping is one of my favourite tools in the customer experience kit, but perhaps not for the reasons you may think. While it is known most prominently for helping organisations better understand and improve the granular levels of customer experience, if done well, it can significantly impact nurturing a customer-centric culture and bringing the organisation together.

If you're a customer experience leader or work in a customer experience capacity, you will likely be quite familiar with customer journey mapping. However, over my years as a practitioner, I've noticed that no company conducts customer journey mapping the same way. So, in this section, I aim to provide a consolidated view of what, in my opinion, are the best practices for utilising customer journey mapping within your organisation to maximise the benefits.

I practice two core disciplines. I'll start with **Retrospective Customer Journey Mapping**, which examines an existing (as-is) customer journey to understand precisely what your customer experiences, find and mitigate friction, and build on positive moments that matter.

For retrospective customer journey mapping, you need as much data and insight as possible.

The ideal scenario is that you can map the entire customer journey with actual data points that show you know exactly what is happening within each customer interaction rather than making assumptions about what you **think** is happening with each customer interaction.

There is a vast wealth of data and insight that you can use to build your retrospective customer journey map. Below is an example list, and by all means, this is not exhaustive. You should, of course, use relevant data to your business and your unique customer experience, but here's a starter for ten:

- Customer feedback from surveys
- Conversational analytics and sentiment data
- Customer testimonials
- Social listening (e.g. Instagram, Facebook and TikTok)
- Online review platforms (e.g. Trust Pilot and TripAdvisor)
- Complaints and compliments
- User data (e.g. how a customer interacts with your product, service, physical store or website)
- Internal operational measures (e.g. KPIs and SLAs)
- Employee insight (voice of the employee, VoE): this is often overlooked, but your employees are usually a gold mine of customer insight

If you are looking at this list and shaking your head, thinking that you don't have any of the data, then take this as a call to action and make it a top task to introduce listening posts and data collection points.

And if you are in that position of minimal data and insight, it doesn't mean that customer journey mapping isn't a viable option for you; it just means that you will have to build your customer journey map using your and your team's insight, which may include bias and ultimately won't present the most accurate view of your customer experience.

However, this is an okay starting place because, culturally, it will at least get you to start thinking more deeply about your customer experience and enable you to identify every data gap you have.

You can do this by asking these questions at each interaction within the customer journey;

"Do I think this happens, or do I know this happens?"

"Do I think the customer feels this way, or do I know the customer feels this way?" and

"Do I think this is what the customer wants and expects or do I know this is what the customer wants and expects?"

If you think rather than know, then, of course, you are making assumptions, and I'd recommend that you start collecting data for each of these points in the customer journey.

Let's walk through my recommended process for **retrospective customer journey mapping**.

Step One: Identify The Customer Journey You Plan To Map

You will have a high-level customer journey, something which follows the lines of;

- **Product and service awareness**
- **Onboarding**
- **Purchase**
- **Delivery, support or after-care**
- **Exit**

This high-level view will be different depending on your type of business. Still, generally speaking, you should be able to identify the high-level phases a customer will experience while interacting with you.

Now, it is valuable to journey map this high-level experience because that will give you a high-level overview of which phase requires attention at any given moment in time. Still, the most value will come from looking at each journey phase more closely. Why?

As I explained at the beginning of this section, customer journey mapping enables a granular view, so this process value is maximised when you get specific.

So, before you get started, you need to identify which customer journey you'll be mapping on this occasion to enable clarity for everybody involved.

You could map a problematic part of the journey, such as an abandoned cart or a complaint.

You could also map your most profitable customer journey, where you see the highest value per transaction.

Alternatively, you could explore your least-known customer journey, where you recently implemented a process change and want to understand how customers interact with it.

It's also essential to define the journey's parameters, specifically its start and end. This isn't always black and white; for example, a business-to-business (B2B) company might start reviewing its ticket management system when it receives a customer query. However, it could go back further and consider the point of failure within the journey mapping.

There isn't a right or wrong answer here; regardless of where the review starts and ends, it needs to be defined.

Step One In Action: Customer Journey Mapping (And Management) In Finance

I previously designed and managed a customer journey mapping program for a large finance company. The customer experience team chose one new customer journey to map each month.

The journey we mapped each month was selected at the business's request, as the team received an influx of requests from departments all over the company to gain a deeper insight into their part of the customer experience.

The team reviewed the requests and prioritised the pipeline to align with the broader operational and strategic priorities.

"Receive an influx of requests"... It sounds like the CX team was in high demand, right? Integral?

Well, yes, it was, but it didn't start that way. Initially, the team had to knock on doors and self-choose which journeys to map. We had to do the work and prove the value before the wider business started taking an interest in this odd visualisation of the customer and their feelings. Still, we did do the job, and the wider business did see and feel the benefit, and by the time I moved on two years later, the program was very much in demand.

Step Two: Identify The Customer Persona

Once your customer journey is identified, you must decide which customer persona you will map the experience of.

This step may be more critical for some customer journeys than others. Still, it's valuable to consider your customer journey through each different customer persona lens because each of your customer personas may have different wants, needs and, therefore, experiences.

For example, you may have a Gen Z persona group that can easily navigate your website and understand the self-help support provided by your knowledge base without the need to access live chat for additional support. Even if they did need to access live chat, they may be very comfortable with this technology.

On the other hand, you might have a Boomer who doesn't find your website navigation particularly intuitive, doesn't want to bother with the self-help knowledge base, and would prefer to speak to somebody instantly on the phone rather than faff around with a live chat.

While your policy and process may be the same for both of these customer persona examples, the ultimate experience each has will be different. Understanding these differences is essential for designing accordingly. Although you might start by mapping the journey for one particular persona, repeating this process for all your customer personas is beneficial.

If you don't yet have customer personas, it would be worthwhile for you to pause customer journey mapping and focus on developing customer personas first.

Step Two In Action: Customer Journey Mapping (And Management) In Finance

As soon as the team confirmed which experience they would map that month, they would go on the hunt for data. Data was in relative abundance at this company, so upon the gathering of data, the team would identify which customer personas were most valuable to map.

In this instance, the team usually reviewed around twenty unique customer journeys and fully progressed to map an average of five per month.

These five fully mapped customer journeys usually represent the persona/s most impacted by the experience, and comparisons would be made to understand any particular nuances that need to be considered.

Step Three: Gather Your Intelligence

OK, so you might have noticed that 'step two in action' (above) references collecting the data before deciding on the customer persona.

Yet, it is here in step three that I am advising you to gather your intelligence, i.e. data and insight. This approach is flexible. It might be that data, and insight collection are valuable to help you understand which persona is more useful to look at; it might even be that data and insight collection, to some degree, is most useful before you even decide on what customer journey to focus on, so step into this process with a degree of flexibility and work in an order which gets you the best result.

But generally speaking, once you've confirmed your customer journey focus and which persona you are going to walk the shoes off, you will have to either start or grow your data collection at this point; now you know what you're looking for you can go and get it (if you have it). This is where you would hunt for the data points on your aforementioned list:

- Customer feedback from surveys
- Conversational analytics and sentiment data
- Customer testimonials

- Social listening (e.g. Instagram, Facebook and TikTok)
- Online review platforms (e.g. Trust Pilot and TripAdvisor)
- Complaints and compliments
- User data (e.g. how a customer interacts with your product, service, physical store or website)
- Internal operational measures (e.g. KPIs and SLAs)
- Employee insight (voice of the employee, VoE): this is often overlooked, but your employees are usually a gold mine of customer insight

Again, this list isn't exhaustive, but it gives you an idea of the data you can leverage to help build your retrospective customer journey.

At a high level, consider the steps your customer needs to go through and the technology, people, policies, and processes they need to interact with. Then, review what data your business collects in connection with any of these touch points.

This is also an advantageous part of the customer journey mapping process, as it requires communication with all departments involved in your customer journey of focus.

Suppose you're asking a person or department for data. In that case, they will usually want to know why, and here, you can explain your reasons and start a conversation about their engagement during the customer journey review and during the subsequent enhancement work (management) afterwards.

Step Three In Action: Customer Journey Mapping (And Management) In Finance

The CX team would map, at a very high level, the known customer steps to understand what actions the customer needed to take, what tools they had to use, what policy they encountered, and what process guided their journey.

Once they had this visualisation, they could identify the departments they needed to speak to, the people who best understood this part of the experience, and those accountable for its management.

This information enabled the team to seek the required data and insight proactively.

This wasn't always easy.

Sometimes, it was challenging to get, both technically and with barriers from nervous people concerned about the potentially critical magnifying lens.

Sometimes, the data didn't exist or was so limited that it failed to offer accurate customer representation. Regardless, they worked with stakeholders to collect as much insight as possible to map the customer journey to the best of their ability.

Step Four: Map The Journey

We are finally on to the juicy bit.

You know your focus area, you see the persona you will be walking in the shoes of, and you have as much data and insight as you can get your inquisitive little hands on.

Now it's time to get mapping.

Whether you have insight or not, I recommend using empathetic customer journey mapping (which applies to all use cases I'll share in this section).

Empathetic customer journey mapping follows a template which includes reviewing each of these elements;

- **The steps your customer takes**: What they do; for example, a customer looking for product advice may enter your website, type in the search bar, click an option presented, read the text, search for a live chat option, interact with the chat, etc

- **Customer wants:** What the customer wants from each step (for example, if they are typing in your search bar, they may want predictive text input).

- **Customer expectations:** Whilst these can be similar to customer wants, they are worth considering separately as they can differ depending on customer circumstances. For example, a customer using your search bar might want predictive text to recommend search terms, but if they are a returning customer who has found your search function ineffective previously, despite *wanting* predictive text input, they may *expect* not to get it.

- **What actually happens?:** This is the most critical element of the retrospective customer journey map because here, we ask what happens at each point of the journey, despite what the customer wants and expects.

Data and insight are essential because the fewer assumptions we make here, the better. Here, we should be able to (with data) answer questions such as how many search attempts it takes for the customer to get the information they want, how long it takes to read the information they have found, how long and how effortful the entire experience was and what their interaction with the live chat look like, etc.

If the customer's actual experience doesn't meet their wants and expectations, we can clearly recognise a friction point that we need to address as an action item. Are we setting incorrect expectations or simply not meeting expectations as we should?

- **How does the customer feel?:** Within this part, we ask how the customer feels for each step of the customer journey. Do they feel uncertain about something? Are they indifferent? Do they feel frustrated, perhaps surprised, or maybe even joyous?

Like before, we ideally use insight to record how the customer feels, as well as insight from direct customer feedback, conversation analytics and even employee insight.

For example, have we noticed grumbling comments in the

feedback left regarding the self-help (knowledge base) function? Or has the front line shared how customers struggle to access the live chat function?

Recognising customer emotion can help us identify moments that matter and prioritise actions in the improvement pipeline.

If we can see that customers feel most strongly about certain things or specific points within the customer journey, then we must focus our attention.

Think back to the Peak End Rule, in which the most memorable interactions are those in which we feel the most intense emotions. These interactions ultimately cultivate our perception, translating into the customer experience as we know it.

Again, the template you use is somewhat flexible. I recommend this as a baseline, but you can also include motivators and influences.

A top tip for designing your customer journey map template is to consider not only the customer journey but also how you can develop your internal stakeholder's interest, particularly if you recognise that there may be engagement challenges.

One way to successfully do this is to associate financial values with the customer journey, mainly if your stakeholders speak in money.

To do this, at each point of the journey, you would capture all associated costs and income generation, which enables you to recognise where you can become more operationally efficient.

Another way to engage stakeholders is to map the internal journey alongside the customer journey. This is often known as backstage and frontstage.

Backstage is the internal process (frequently, a service blueprint is used here), and you would map elements like the internal people involved, what tools and tech they use, what policy and process they follow and what barriers they meet.

Frontstage is the customer journey map. By placing the backstage and front stage together, you can map the customer experience and directly tie your internal process to it, which helps identify the root cause of customer experience pains and gains.

Once you have your template and approach, you must decide how you map the customer journey. I advocate for a workshop approach; this is where you conduct steps one to three in preparation for mapping the customer journey in a workshop that engages the broader organisation and/ or any relevant stakeholders.

I advocate for a workshop approach because you can gain fantastic stakeholder insight on the customer journey, which otherwise might be missed through desk-based data review.

Workshops create a safe space for exploratory conversation in which you're reviewing the current experience and inspiring conversation for enhancement and innovation that can be captured. Workshops are also a fantastic opportunity to bring people and departments together who might not regularly collaborate, which has the added benefit of breaking down silos, growing an understanding of how ways of working impact each other and cultivating an enhanced way of partnership working.

Suppose you progress with undertaking workshops to complete customer journey mapping, depending on the complexity of the process and the number of stakeholders involved. In that case, you may require more than one workshop per customer journey map.

While these can be done remotely, I have always found that a more profound conversation takes place when conducted in person.

The workshop approach may not be right for you. You may be a Solopreneur, and you would be the only delegate.

Perhaps you don't have the resources available to prioritise regular workshops.

Maybe you are early on this journey, and you don't have the engagement levels you would need to undertake a practical customer journey mapping workshop (yet!).

Whatever the reasons, you don't have to workshop.

The alternative to workshops is to simply sit down in front of your computer (with an Excel spreadsheet, word doc or, if you want to get fancy, a customer journey mapping platform) or with a whiteboard and some Post-it notes and use the template and your data, map the customer journey yourself.

If there are other departments or people involved in this customer journey, before making the finished journey visible to the broader organisation, I'd recommend sharing your output for feedback with them first.

Again, this is great from a relationship perspective as it enables them to feed into the final production and allows them to review and prepare for any subsequent work that the journey generates.

Step Four In Action: Customer Journey Mapping (And Management) In Finance

Despite my recommended approach of utilising workshops to complete the customer journey mapping, we took the alternative approach.

We completed desk-based customer journey mapping during my time at the finance company. The mapping activity was completed by two experts whose roles were dedicated to this task.

The primary rationale behind not workshopping the map production was the fast pace at which we were required to produce output and the high stakeholder engagement they had nurtured through the monthly review process.

Honestly, when we started this initiative, we wouldn't have got the stakeholder buy-in to conduct regular customer journey mapping workshops. However, engagement grew so strongly that we could've changed that process.

Secondary to that rationale was the monthly customer journey mapping review and action forum, which created that safe space for experience exploration, ideas, action planning and reporting, which I'll explain next in step five.

Step Five: Action and Governance

Great, you've completed the customer journey map. Job done, right? Wrong.

Deciding which customer journey to map and which persona to walk in the shoes of, collecting all that data and insight, chatting with relevant stakeholders and producing the final customer journey map output was the easy bit.

You might have noted that I've referred to customer journey mapping… and management. This is because customer journey mapping is really just the beginning; the mapping serves the purpose of understanding the customer experience, of really flipping the internal and often operational view on its head, and instead looking at the experience with an outside-in view, through the customer's eyes.

This deeper understanding enables you to look at the experience holistically, identify friction and pain points, and the parts that drive the most satisfaction…

to see, hear and feel what the customer sees, hears and feels.

But we have yet to come on to the 'management'. The management of the experience is where you turn insight into action.

When you reach the point where you have designed an intentional customer experience, you should potentially have a long list of actions that focus on the following:

- **Removing those friction points**
- **Eliminating the gap between expectations and unmet expectations**
- **Driving forward with the innovative ideas that have been generated**
- **Reducing insight gaps**
- **Changing metrics and success measures (if what you have is no longer fit for purpose)**
- **Conducting even deeper dives (if you feel you have only scratched the surface)**

Depending on the size of your organisation, these actions may be performed by just a few or spread across multiple departments. Either way, they require strong governance to ensure a robust approach to evolving and managing the journey.

At a minimum, I recommend that one person be accountable for the entire customer journey mapping program. This person is responsible for completing customer journey maps and their end output, governing the ongoing management, and, ideally, completing the actions derived and agreed upon.

There should be a place to capture and track all of the agreed actions, the accountable people, timelines and updates, etc (general task management), and they should be a central place to discuss and track progress.

A place such as a monthly forum could be a standalone meeting with stakeholders focusing on nothing but the customer journey mapping process, or it may be on the agenda within part of another already established and relevant meeting.

An integral part of the customer journey management process is establishing appropriate success measures and metrics. After all it's a lot of work to do, it's key to ensure the resource you are committing is driving the improvements you have to achieve.

Sometimes, our actions don't result in the experience improvements we anticipated; sometimes, we misinterpret the insight and just don't make significant enough changes.

A great way to continually measure progress while utilising the proper measures and metrics is to remap the customer journey constantly. In six months, have we closed the gaps? Have the friction points identified been removed? Are there more vigorous, more impactful and more frequent positive moments that matter?

An ongoing customer journey mapping program is an

excellent way to quality assure the customer experience you deliver. It's also a way to keep a continually high level of experience and understanding. After all, we quality assure so many elements of our business, why not the customer experience?

Step Five In Action: Customer Journey Mapping (And Management) In Finance

I mentioned in step four that during my time with the finance company, we held a monthly customer journey mapping review and action forum; in my opinion, this is where the real organisational change occurred.

When the team first started the journey mapping program, it was hard to gain traction from stakeholders. Everybody was busy. They all had huge to-do lists and to ask them to spend extra time looking at customer journey maps (of experience they felt like they knew inside and out) was a hard thing to sell.

But I knew how important it was to engage the wider business because real change certainly wouldn't happen from a tiny department alone. The improvement actions and change decisions needed to be owned by the right people.

So, despite a lack of initial engagement, a monthly forum was set up, and all senior leaders, managers and people influential to the journey we were mapping were invited to review the output and take ownership of actions.

In the beginning, few people came. In the end, we didn't have enough chairs in the room to accommodate everybody. We didn't have enough space. It was amazing. Stakeholders from all over the business began to see the real benefit that this new, magnified lens had. Their own insight grew, and they started to see this resource as a valuable way to refine and develop the part of the customer journey that they had the most influence on.

The forum was not only a place to share the customer journey outputs but it was a place for honest, confident and bold discussion. It was a place where we critically analysed why we did what we did. We challenged people to think about how we could do things differently.

Stakeholders, with the help of the wider group, came up with solutions and actions that needed to take place to make the changes that we could all see where required.

These forums weren't always smooth sailing; there were challenges and disagreements, but ultimately, the conversation drove positive change.

Each month, stakeholders would give updates on their actions and share the progress that was or wasn't made with the group. This held us all accountable, and this approach to governance drove the initiative's success.

At the beginning of this section, I said that customer journey mapping nurtures a customer-centric culture. This is how. This shared approach, joint ownership, and collaborative conversations...these drove a customer-centric mindset and helped us shift from an inside-out, operational view to an outside-in, customer-focused view.

That's retrospective customer journey mapping covered (looking at the current, 'as is' experience). Let's look at **proactive customer journey mapping**.

Proactive customer journey mapping is the process of mapping a new customer experience. You will use this approach if you are creating a brand new product or service, opening a new store or restaurant, using new customer-impacting technology or changing the customer experience in some other way.

By using customer journey mapping up front, you are proactively designing the experience your customers want and expect. You deliberately design the experience to ensure you meet their demands and expectations and cultivate the experience with intent.

For proactive customer journey mapping, you would follow

the same approach as retrospective customer journey mapping; however, you may not have access to as much data (especially if it is a brand-new experience rather than an altered experience). So here you are, relying on your and your team's knowledge and insight, market research and customer research to identify your customers wants, needs and drivers.

Let's use a restaurant example to illustrate proactive customer journey mapping. Without mapping the journey, you may design a restaurant experience that makes total sense on paper. Customers book online through a third-party booking system, turn up on time, order via a QR code, eat, pay using the QR code, leave, and receive a feedback request.

But if you map the customer journey, examine each step critically, and imagine yourself in your new customers' shoes, you might spot improvement opportunities.

For example, what if the third-party booking system requires a customer to set up an account, and your customer doesn't want to do that—they just want to make a quick booking?

This action could be a source of frustration and cause customer drop-off.

What if your customers come to the restaurant thirty minutes earlier than their reservation because they want a drink first? Are the restaurant space and staffing resources set up to facilitate that?

What if customers don't want to use a QR code to access the menu? What if they prefer a physical menu? And what if they don't want to pay using the QR code because they would rather pay in cash? Has the heavy use of technology been considered concerning the reduction in human interaction and the impact that it will have on the customer experience and their desire to return?

The initial experience design looks good on paper. However, if you dig deeper to understand what the experience looks and feels like for your customer, you can avoid costly design mistakes and even spot opportunities to differentiate from your competition.

Proactive customer journey mapping should be commonplace within your company, regardless of size or industry. The best practice is to design your experience up front and then start a programme of retrospective customer journey mapping when you are up and running to ensure the experience you deliver is as you intended and to recognise any change required.

Growing Your

Culture
Membrane

Growing your Culture Membrane

So far, each section in the book has been focused on developing a deeper understanding of customer experience.

It's explored the significant value of that deep understanding and the importance of intentional customer experience design and management, going beyond what's typically seen in operational practice.

This book started by stating that CX-Ism is a philosophy that redefines business success, where customer experience isn't just a strategy you implement—but a movement you lead. To that point, the book's final parts will focus more explicitly on the leading.

All of the theory and practical content that we have covered so far is aimed at ultimately strengthening your culture, and it requires a level of leadership and accountability to ensure that happens.

However, for real change to occur, for organisational-wide understanding and individual accountability, there must be a membrane. A living sheath, connecting every customer experience-focused action. Communication between activities, people, and departments needs to be nurtured, and your efforts must be protected and strengthened.

Consider the following section's advice on how to grow your customer experience leadership membrane.

Are Your

Values And
Behaviours

Aligned?

Are Your Values And Behaviours Aligned?

Let's start this culture membrane growth with a reality check: An honest and critical reflection on your current organisational culture.

Ask yourself these questions and answer with sincerity.

Do you have clear organisational ambitions, such as values? A customer vision? A customer promise? A mission statement?

If you do, does everyone in the organisation know what they are?

If they do, does everyone in the organisation believe in them?

Let me guess how you answered.
1. **Yes**
2. **Maybe**
3. **No**

Most companies, in some form or another, have a North Star, or a few.

Business owners and leaders understand that to try and keep the company on track, aligned and motivated, and true to their customers and stakeholders, there needs to be guiding principles.

These typically come in the form of organisational values, customer visions and promises, and a mission statement. Failing those, there is often at least a strategy.

Being confident that everyone in the organisation knows what these are becomes less common than having them. A lack of company-wide understanding, whether you are a two-person operation or a two-hundred-person operation, can occur for a latitude of reasons.

It might be as simple as the company just not sharing these widely enough or communicating them well. They could be extended, complex, and just too complicated for individuals to remember.

Even worse, it could be that they change so often that individuals can't keep up with the messaging (this is not a good place to be).

And even if everyone does know them, let's say they are literally plastered to the walls, floating around screensavers and quoted on the mugs. Does your company believe in them? More often than not, if you are being really honest and critical, the answer will be no.

How often do you hear employees or maybe even your friends and family, when talking about their work environments, say things like, *"I'm expected to do A, B and C, but how on earth am I supposed to do it when this system keeps failing…if they really cared they would sort this out."*

Replace the word 'system' with 'technology', 'policy' or 'process', and you get the gist.

All too often, our people face barriers to carrying out their daily responsibilities effectively, which, over time, if the barriers aren't mitigated, starts to reflect on how seriously individuals believe the company takes the values/visions/mission statements, etc.

It's the old 'practice what you preach' mentality, if leadership isn't seen to actively care, then the broader organisation will struggle to believe that they are more than words on a page.

From a cultural perspective, if your ambition is to nurture and nourish customer experience and make it a movement that drives your business success (and it should be), this misalignment can not be present. Your answers to those questions need to be:

1. Yes

2. Yes

3. Yes (Oh, HECK YES!)

Schein's Organisational Culture Model is a great tool to help you achieve definitive answers to those three questions, and once you have the answers, you can start to work to strengthen your culture through that much-desired company cohesion.

Schein's model is valuable in recognising the deep-rooted

cultural drivers or inhibitors that your organisation may have.

Many companies who struggle to embed customer experience into their DNA fail to recognise that this is more than skin-deep (skin being the strategy).

It's common to throw resources at a voice of the customer programmes, a journey mapping programme, a bit of training here, and an accreditation there: these are all valuable and admirable actions, but unless there is a strong customer-centric culture enveloping this strategy, the impact and benefits will be short-lived.

Schein's Organisational Culture Model recognises three layers of culture:

Artefacts

These are visible and tangible elements of culture—like customer-centric slogans, weekly CSAT reporting, or CX dashboards on the wall for all to see.

In some companies, cultural elements can even be seen in how employees dress. I'll never forget a story a friend shared; she worked in the UK for a Japanese-owned technology company.

One year, she had the exciting opportunity to visit the office in Japan. Whilst she loved the experience, she recognised that she stood out like a sore thumb from when she arrived. There she stood, dressed in bold, bright colours and easily identified as an outsider amongst the ocean of black suits floating around her.

The historic culture of this company was stoic and serious, and whilst around the world in other company locations, that was changing, it was still very prevalent in Japan.

Artefacts can be misleading, though.

Just because you have a customer-centric slogan on your mug doesn't mean you believe it.

Just because you report on CSAT doesn't mean it's a valid measure.

Ok, there's a lovely dashboard on the wall with your customer experience performance updated in real-time, does anyone look at it?

As with the Japanese suit story, just because one geographic location has that culture, it may not represent the entire organisation.

Espoused Values

These are the organisation's stated values, such as putting the customer at the heart of decisions, putting the customer first or designing around the needs of our consumers.

Espouse means to adopt or support, so an espoused value is an organisational/individual adopted value, it's a choice.

Espoused values are what artefacts lead from. Where a company says it will put the customer at the heart of its decisions, then a result (artefact) of this might be using a customer-focused measure like CSAT and placing customer-focused performance dashboards on the wall.

However, just because the value is written on the mug, the measure is visible, and the dashboard shines bright doesn't mean that the customer is truly at the heart of all the company's decisions.

If leadership is just walking the walk without talking the talk, we have a culture problem. Quite frankly, there is zero point in the values if they aren't brought to life at all levels, and one of the most significant cultural barriers creating this problem is where the underlying assumptions of a company differ from the espoused values.

Underlying Assumptions

These are the subconscious beliefs that dictate how the organisation actually operates. An easy example to highlight this point is if employees believe that financial performance will always outweigh customer satisfaction, their actions will be to drive financial performance and not customer satisfaction metrics.

Underlying assumptions can be more subtle. I've worked with organisations where they believe the customer doesn't know what they want. This puts the espoused value of customer-centric design on a back foot because if you believe you know better than the customer, you aren't really customer-centric in your design.

I've also worked with companies who believed they couldn't influence the customer experience when something out of their control happened. This results in not fully designing around customer needs, which not only misses huge opportunities to influence customer experience but creates a gap between the espoused value and reality.

There is a conflict where the espoused values are not clearly supported and aligned with the company's underlying assumptions. This conflict damages the culture and will inhibit the success of any customer experience initiative you have.

Ultimately, customer experience is about more than the customer—it's about creating a culture where employees feel empowered to do the right thing consistently. When that alignment between espoused values and underlying assumptions happens, customer experience becomes more than a strategy—it becomes a movement.

I want to recognise the elephant in the room here.

You might be reading this thinking that it's a complete fantasy and that when you see companies' espoused values and underlying assumptions align, you will eat your hat and buy the unicorn next to you a glass of fairy elixir.

I understand. It feels like a dreamscape, right?

Let's use that example again of a company saying (espoused value) that customer satisfaction is the most important thing, yet the underlying assumption is actually that the company's financial performance is the most important thing.

This is not uncommon, and we're all grown-ups, of course, the company's financial performance will come first for a significant majority of most profit-generating companies.

The company can not survive without financial success, which is unsuitable for its employees or customers.

So when we talk about espoused values and underlying assumptions, it's important to understand that these two do not have to be, and likely won't be, one and the same.

But they do have to align, complement and work in tandem.

So, your employees should not feel that it's a matter of customer satisfaction versus financial performance. Instead, they should understand that customer satisfaction is vital to the company because it drives enhanced financial performance.

Your people should see with absolute clarity how your espoused values and underlying assumptions connect, the value of both of them and through everyday decision-making and actions that these are being nurtured and brought to life.

Schein's model was developed in the 1980s; it's about as

old as I am, so it's fair to say that it has needed to evolve and consider new external influences. His original thinking suggested that culture was somewhat linear, with those three layers being rather sterile, clean and hierarchical.

This linear modality also indicated that change could only be achieved slowly, with one layer eventually having a compound effect on the other. However, plenty of agile companies move at a fast pace, and we have seen, for good and bad, how quickly culture can change.

Schein didn't rest on his original success; he saw how businesses' inner workings changed and later updated his work to recognise cultural evolution with particular attention to the importance of leadership in intentionally shaping culture.

Everything in this book so far, whether you are a leader or not, is here to help you shape your culture.

I find Schein's model to be an excellent culture assessment and highly advocate its use no matter where you are in the cycle.

If you are just starting out on a customer experience transformation, great, undertake an assessment.

If you are battling with maintaining momentum, okay, undertake an assessment.

If your efforts are failing, and it's all going to s**t, stop what you are doing immediately and undertake an assessment.

By recognising where the weaknesses lie within your culture, you can take action to strengthen those areas, nurture that culture and create a safe environment (a protective membrane if you will) to undertake successful and long-lasting change successfully.

Put Theory Into Practice

Get Started

Use Schein's model to identify your organisational artefacts, espoused values and underlying assumptions.

Conduct employee and stakeholder workshops, surveys, and interviews to gather insight into these hidden beliefs.

It can be really helpful to bring in an independent facilitator for this entire process as this not only enables employees to be more candid with an independent supporter but also prevents a biased influence from an internal process leader.

Get Critical

Look at your collected insight and highlight the gaps.

Where do words and actions look artificial? Is there meaning behind your words, meaning which resonates with your company? Where do words lack action? Where do beliefs need to be strengthened? Is there transparency and understanding behind your underlying assumptions?

Ask challenging and thought-provoking questions, and workshop this through with your leadership team and organisational representatives: really pull up the sheets.

Don't Overcomplicate It

Deep-rooted change won't take effect overnight, so consistency is required over time.

Show progress as soon as it starts happening, that very action in itself positively nurtures culture. Launch visible, small initiatives—such as team recognition programs or customer feedback showcases—so employees can see change happening in real-time.

I personally like to challenge teams with a marginal gains activity. Marginal gains are the idea that small actions lead to significant change, such as a single water droplet rippling out to eventually create a giant wave. For this activity, it is as simple as asking a team to think of a slight improvement action they can take each day, record it, and evaluate its impact at the end of one month, two months, or three months.

This is a great team activity that everyone can take part in. It's a great way to empower people and show them the power they have to influence change. Obviously, it's a great way to improve your customer experience.

Ensure Visible Action From Leadership

In my book, cultural change can only happen with a top-down and bottom-up effort, but I believe this starts with action from the leadership team. Leaders must visibly demonstrate that customer experience is a non-negotiable part of the business, and they need to show its value through investment: time, money, and resources dedicated to it consistently.

In my work with an international airport, I saw exemplary practice of this.

They embarked on a brand new approach to customer experience and kick-started the work with the framework of a customer experience strategy, customer segmentation, persona creation, a customer vision and customer journey mapping.

This work isn't particularly unusual, but the fact that workshop delegates comprised the entire senior leadership team, including the CEO and the non-exec directors, was unusual. This level of top-down action is a strong and visible indicator of the organisation's commitment.

On the flip side, I have seen customer experience leaders struggle to get into the boardroom, which, without saying, considerably slows progress.

Monitor and Adapt

Culture isn't static (as Schein grew to value the importance of more over the years). Regularly measure the alignment between espoused values and actual behaviours using pulse surveys, feedback loops, and performance reviews. If gaps persist, revisit the assumptions driving them by repeating these five action steps.

Embedding customer experience into culture isn't a one-time effort—it's a journey of aligning beliefs and values. You must consistently follow this up with customer-focused actions to create a movement that drives business success.

Give Your People What They Need To
Succeed

Give Your People What They Need To Succeed: Autonomy, Relatedness And Competence (ARC)

How do you motivate your workforce to buy into, care for, and take action that aligns with your customer experience efforts?

Well, according to the Self-Determination Theory (SDT), we are motivated when these three simple-sounding psychological needs are satisfied:

Autonomy: The need to feel in control

Relatedness: Feeling connected to and understanding the purpose of our work

Competence: A feeling of being capable

If you are an astute reader, you may have spotted that most, if not all, of the theories I have shared in this book originated in the 80's, and the Self-Determination Theory is no different.

Despite being a child of the 80s, I promise this inclusion of '80s business fodder isn't intentional; it simply seems to be the case that a lot of smart-minded business folk, psychologists and behaviourists developed some pretty good theories that are still kicking around today, and SDT is one of them.

It's no surprise either when you think about it, really. If your employees feel autonomous and in control, then they feel trusted. If they feel relatedness, connected to the work they are doing and have a sense of purpose, then it's likely that they enjoy their work and feel their own intrinsic value. Then, to top it off, they feel competent that they can actually do their job, so there is likely to be little worry and self-doubt.

It's a simple-sounding list indeed but if you can support your employees to achieve these psychological needs, then you have developed a naturally self-powered motivation machine.

What I find most appealing about the STD framework, and why I find it so valuable for developing a customer experience culture, is that it drives intrinsic motivation.

Intrinsic motivation is defined as the motivation to engage in a behaviour because of the inherent satisfaction of the activity rather than the desire for a reward or specific outcome. We simply enjoy an activity or see it as an opportunity to explore, learn, and actualise our potential.*

This type of motivation, intrinsic motivation, not only encourages employees to buy in, care and align, but it actually goes a little further, supporting people to adopt new behaviours and even go that extra mile when they see the opportunity to do so.

*According to Introduction to Psychology: Gateways to Mind and Behavior With Concept Maps by Dennis Coon.

This is so important in customer experience because if our people are intrinsically motivated and find their work naturally rewarding, then they are likely to generate novel ideas, fascinating solutions and creative answers to solve challenges.

I often refer to customer experience folk as friction finders. It isn't a term that originated from me, and I'm sorry not to be able to credit who I first heard this from (I can't recall), but it really instead works because, generally speaking, customer experience teams use data and insight to find friction and then support the organisation to eliminate it.

If these teams are intrinsically motivated to smooth this friction, then they will be more likely to find innovative ways to do so, not only fixing the problem but actually improving the customer experience too (we touched on this already in the 'Stuck In The Status Quo' section).

Not only that, but consider the front-line, where quite often they are required to think fast and act quickly to resolve a customers problem. If they enjoy their role and are intrinsically motivated then they will be more inclined to explore the customer issue further, ask question, understand it and use their noggin to think outside the box and provide a customer-centric solution.

Put Theory Into Practice

Part of your efforts to develop and nurture your customer-centric culture should be to encourage intrinsic motivation within your teams, and there are plenty of tactical things you can do.

Allow Autonomy

You hired all of your employees for a reason, because they have something to offer the company and you trust in them to turn up and do what's required.

So TRUST them.

Give them the freedom to make decisions about their work. This fosters a sense of ownership and responsibility.

You can do this by engaging them in activities like we have already discussed. Use customer journey mapping as an example, involve them in the process, gather their insight and ask them what they think you can do to enhance the experience.

You can also use flexible process and policy. Okay, all companies have a way of doing things and to a degree, that's a necessity, there needs to be some structure otherwise everything could well go to pot.

But create flexibility in your process and policy to enable your people to bend and adapt, within reason, but as they see fit, in order to do the right thing.

On top of this, if s policy or process just isn't working in the best way it can, make sure your team know that their voice, their feedback can influence change.

Creatively Challenge

Assign tasks that are appropriately challenging to keep employees engaged and promote growth.

The word appropriate is important here because each employee will have their own desire for growth, some will want more, some will want less. I talked about a marginal gains activity in the last section, thats a simple customer experience growth challenge for everyone.

Challenge your team to be curious too. Curiosity sparks creativity so build a team who asks why things are done in certain ways and who challenge the status quo. To do this, create a safe space for open curiosity to thrive.

I have used dedicated **Replay Sessions** for this, where we would gather a team and all listen to a customer service call, or read a policy, or review a customer interaction and we would critically analyses it. Together, a room full of stakeholders of different levels and from different departments coming together to think creatively.

This is a easy but fantastically effective way to encourage collaboration between teams and people who don't usually work with each other, challenge, grow and share control.

Recognise And Reward

This should go without saying really, but I'll say it anyway, recognise and reward your people for the awesome things they do.

In the world of customer experience we see this most commonly applied to a voice of the customer framework, whereby customers provide feedback and the company has a recognition system attached.

I've worked with a few company which had monthly awards connected to direct customer feedback, in which each month, using some pre-determined criteria, a handful of employees would be recognised for the awesome feedback their efforts generated. They would get their name on the CX wall of fame and a token thank you gift.

But your recognition can come in many forms and even a simplo thank you can go a long way.

Interestingly, if you nurture and intrinsically motivated workforce you have to apply an enhanced level of consideration to rewards as researchers have found the **Over Justification Effect** (nothing is ever simple is it!?! Eat dark chocolate, don't eat dark chocolate. Drink red wine, don't drink red wine. Reward your team, don't reward your team!).

The Over Justification Effect occurs when extrinsic motivation is applied (like a physical reward) and the person you are rewarding ends up feeling less intrinsically motivated as they question their own motivation.

Eat the chocolate. Drink the red wine. Reward where you see fit.

Ultimately, Self-Determination Theory supports your mission to make customer experience a movement. It motivates employees to buy-in, to care and to strive for customer experience excellence, day in, day out with a naturally intrinsic motivation.

Self-Determination Theory cultivates an environment where your teams don't just do what they're told—they want to deliver an exceptional experience.

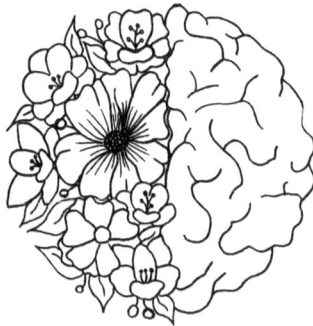

Nudge Nudge

Nudge Nudge

Do you have a fitness app on your phone? Or a calorie counter? Or a brain training app? Or some kind of habit tracker?

If you do, I bet it sends you notifications throughout the day to complete a workout, track your food, finish the puzzle, or track your habits.

Do you set yourself reminders on Alexa?

Do you leave little notes around the house for yourself or your partner?

Or strategically place items to act as a reminder to do something?

Do you keep your fruit bowl visible to encourage the family to pick a piece of fruit for a snack?

Do you leave the books you read or want to read on the coffee table?

If you do, these are all nudges—sometimes subtle, sometimes less so, but nudges nonetheless.

Nudges act as little reminders to keep information prominent in your memory and promote immediate actions or changes in your behaviour.

Notifications and reminders are needed until you form a strong enough habit that you no longer need an active reminder; they just become a natural part of your behaviour.

We all tend to use nudges in our day-to-day lives to guide our behaviour without too heavy of a dictatorial type order.

It's funny how our psychology works in this sense, and it's probably easiest to share an example we all recognise through a stereotypical parent-child interaction. The parent orders a child to tidy their room, but the child sullenly declines. Yet, if the parent drops into the conversation about how wonderful it is that the child's sibling tidies their room, the child might just take it upon themselves to pick up a few toys without even being asked.

This quirk of our psychology remains with us throughout our life.

Psychologically, we tend to respond better to gentle encouragement because it preserves our sense of autonomy. When we have a choice, we're more likely to engage positively with a behaviour.

This preference for being nudged rather than ordered is rooted in our aforementioned intrinsic motivation and desire for self-determination. This is why nudges, which feel more like friendly suggestions or are sometimes so subtle that they are only recognised in our subconscious, are often more effective.

Step in Nudge Theory!

Nudge Theory was popularised in 2008 by Richard Thaler and Cass Sunstein in their 2008 book, "Nudge: Improving Decisions About Health, Wealth, and Happiness." (Finally, a theory from the naughties rather than the 80s!).

They drew on behavioural economics and psychology insights, which have been floating around for years. Daniel Kahneman (Mr Peak End Rule) and Amos Tversky did a lot of foundational work on cognitive biases and decision-making (this was primarily developed in the 70s and 80s. Oh.), which showed how small changes in how choices are presented could significantly influence behaviour. Their work significantly impacted future research and supports what is now well known as the Nudge theory.

Nudge theory is about subtly guiding people's choices without restricting their freedom.

Done well, it typically utilises small environmental cues or changes to encourage a desired behaviour. For instance, placing particular food at eye level in a supermarket to subtly encourage customers to buy them. This is such a successful tactic that brands pay a premium for such supermarket placement. No one forces customers to select these items, but because they are so prominent, it's more likely that they will.

The success of the Nudge theory is that it's easy to opt out, but the nudge makes the desired action more likely.

Nudge Theory is incredibly common in the business world, particularly in sales and marketing; if you become aware of it, you can easily recognise it. For example, you may be purchasing something, and the text on the screen says, 'Hurry, there are only three items left.' This is one of the less subtle nudges, but a nudge it is.

You can see it in other areas, too. Hotels, for example, usually aim to operate more cost-efficiently and more environmentally sustainably, so they are driven to reduce the volumes of laundry they wash. They don't order customers to reuse their towels but leave cards in the room highlighting the environmental benefits of reusing a towel. More often than not, hotel guests will opt to reuse their towels. Nudge.

You can also see it in customer experience. A popular example is Disney's (gosh, I can't believe this is the first time I talk about Disney in a book about Customer Experience!) approach in their theme parks. They subtly manipulate guest behaviour to reduce wait times and improve flow. They use signs and elaborately dressed staff members to nudge guests toward less crowded areas or attractions, effectively managing the crowd without guests even realising it. They use estimated ride wait times (now in the form of a handy app) to help guests plan their day around the park. To guests, this feels like a choice, that they have ownership, but in reality, their choices have been quite cleverly directed. Still, this improves the overall customer experience by making their visit more enjoyable.

However, I've included Nudge Theory in the culture section.

While you can and should use this theory in your customer experience design, I'm focusing on its internal use:

How you can use It to drive change and enable customer experience to become more than an initiative or strategy but an actual movement throughout your entire organisation.

Part of the success in making customer experience a movement is the continued visibility and palpable feeling of customer experience, everywhere. It needs to infiltrate conversation at all levels; it needs to be seen, heard and felt. It can not just be a round of training, a monthly feature in a report or an annual awards submission.

I've worked with several companies over the years with an explicit focus on customer experience training, and each of them utilised a version of nudge theory to support the extended benefit of that training.

Some progressed with the follow-up use of CULTIVATE CX-TV, bespoke regular video content aimed at specific organisational needs. This is popped straight into the employee's inbox (or embedded into the learning management system) and provides monthly customer experience stimulation and message reinforcement (A rather big nudge).

Others utilised a post-training behaviour implementation strategy such as a to-do list of customer experience management good practices (which includes advice like sharing customer feedback in every daily standup, making the customer performance metric visible and updating it daily and sharing customer experience top tips in a shared company-wide, digital whiteboard).

Both options are ways that these companies promote customer experience, conversation, and action without autocratic commands.

I have another fun and creative example of nudge theory. I attended a company conference as the keynote speaker. The conference was focused on launching the company's new, very customer-centric values. It was heart-themed, with the slogan 'Customers at the heart of everything'. The conference was one big nudge, and they played heart-themed music throughout the day. It was an impactful day, and the memory of that day, the big and little nudges, will have a long-lasting impact on the delegates.

Put Theory Into Practice

To use Nudge Theory internally to develop a culture that centres around customer experience, there really is no end to what you can do. Get creative! But as a starting point, here's a few things to consider:

Visual Cues

Use posters, screensavers, or dashboards that promote customer-centric values and success stories.

Keep them fresh and updated.

In a few companies I have consulted with, we have placed new monthly customer journey maps on the wall, warts and all. That really kept the CX conversation alive!

Remember that, according to Schein's Organisational Culture Model, these are known as artefacts. To be effective, they must reflect your company's espoused values and underlying assumptions.

Training Modules

Incorporate nudge principles into training to encourage desired behaviours. Don't just have explicit stand-alone customer experience training modules. Customer experience is influenced by every single area of your business, so intertwine it into every training module.

Feedback Loops

This should be a given, but provide regular, positive feedback to reinforce customer-focused actions. Share feedback with your team, not just feedback but also what action the company has taken regarding the input and what benefit it has driven. Use a good old 'You said, We did' approach.

Recognition Programs

Highlight and reward customer-focused behaviour to reinforce its importance.

By consistently applying these nudges, you can create a culture where customer experience becomes second nature.

Nudge theory is perhaps one of the most straightforward additions to your culture development approach. Make it part of your culture membrane.

" Most people can do awe-inspiring things. Sometimes they just need a little nudge. "

Tim Ferriss - Entrepreneur

Make
Customer Experience
A
Movement

Make Customer Experience A Movement

The success of your business doesn't lie in your products, services, pricing or marketing. It lies in the emotions of each and every one of your customers.

Every interaction and every touchpoint is not just a transaction but a moment of connection. CX-Ism shows us that business success isn't earned through short-term wins but by the long-term emotional connections we create.

This isn't a romantic fantasy or a marketing gimmick—it's the reality of business, any business, all businesses, your business.

In today's challenging, competitive and fast paced world, businesses that rely only on short-term wins or transactional thinking will be left behind. But those that place emotional connection at their core will thrive in ways others can't.

Let this knowledge fuel the movement within your organisation, transforming customer experience from an operational effort into a lasting legacy of growth, connection, and shared purpose.

The future of your business isn't built on what you sell, but on how your customers feel when they choose you. Lead the movement. Redefine success.

CX-ISM

A philosophy that redefines business success, where customer experience isn't just a strategy you implement—but a movement you lead.

Happy CX-ing,

Katie

About The Author

Katie Stabler
**Founder and Director of CULTIVATE
Customer Experience by Design**

Katie spent over a decade in the not-for-profit sector, supporting organisations with the most vulnerable customers to deliver a beautifully curated experience.

She then spent two years working for one of Europe's largest credit management companies driving their Customer Experience Strategy forward within a fantastic leadership team.

Here, she became a Customer Experience Professional Association (CXPA) member and a Certified Customer Experience Professional (CCXP).

In 2019 Katie decided to step out of the heavily regulated (FCA) finance industry and move into the digital/e-commerce world joining an International membership organisation as the Head of Customer Experience and Member Optimisation.

In 2020 Katie founded CULTIVATE! Katie utilises a commercially astute, balanced approach to help organisations develop and adopt a profitable customer experience strategy. Katie's clear, conscientious and creative ability to engage enables her to work across all levels of the business supporting cultural (and digital) transformation. Gathering and using data, Katie drives real action from insight, delivering tangible results.

Katie co-authored the Amazon No#1 best seller 'Customer Experience 2', is named one of the top five Global CX Thought Leaders in 2024. She is the host of the Awards International Customer Experience Awards, daytime celebrations.

Katie regularly contributes to professional publications and speaks at conferences around the world including Latvia, Dublin, India the UK and Greece.

Katie lives in the beautiful, green, leafy land of Cheshire (UK) and also happens to be a Masterchef UK Quarterfinalist, so is passionate about all things food.

You can contact Katie at
Katie@cultivatecustomerexperience.com

Connect with her on Linkedin (just search for Katie Stabler) and Instagram
@customer experience cultivator

Website:
www.cultivatecustomerexperience.com

Don't forget to leave a review for this book on Amazon and share your thoughts on social media. If you Tag Katie or Cultivate it will be sure to be re-shared.

www.ingramcontent.com/pod-product-compliance
Lightning Source LLC
Chambersburg PA
CBHW070926210326
41520CB00021B/6822